The
Autobiography
of
Benvenuto Cellini

The Autobiography of Benvenuto Cellini

edited by
Alfred Tamarin

Abridged and adapted from the translation
by John Addington Symonds

THE MACMILLAN COMPANY
Collier-Macmillan Ltd., London

The Macmillan Company
Collier-Macmillan Canada, Ltd., Toronto, Ontario

Library of Congress catalog card number: 69–11591

Printed in the United States of America
FIRST PRINTING

introduction

Benvenuto Cellini was probably the greatest goldsmith and jeweler of the sixteenth century. He was also,
as he paints himself in his classic autobiography, an adven-
turer and a brawler, quick to quarrel and, if need be, to
shed blood. Cellini's magnificent creations in gold, silver
and precious stones were the delight of princes and prelates
and were prized ornaments of queens and courtesans. But
Benvenuto dreamed of bigger things, of colossal statues in
marble and bronze which would rank him with the greatest
of the Florentine artists—Leonardo da Vinci and Michelangelo. When Cellini unveiled his bronze masterpiece,
Perseus, which is still standing in Florence, he confidently
expected to be overwhelmed with honors and commissions
to do greater and greater works. Unfortunately, nothing of
the kind materialized. Angry, frustrated and despairing,
Benvenuto Cellini poured his passion into his autobiography and unintentionally ensured for himself the immor-
tality he coveted.

Cellini's autobiography re-creates with unequaled

vividness the Renaissance years during the middle of the sixteenth century in Florence, Rome and Paris. Since he had no intention of flattering princes or glorifying popes, he wrote with a biting force that rings with truth. He had to explain his disappointment, if only to himself. The intensity of his feelings demanded the colorful language of the streets, an ability to etch characterizations in acid and a capacity to capture startling and revealing detail. Cellini's prose was anything but politic, which may explain why the document remained unpublished for more than a century and a half.

Benvenuto realized that he was on perilous ground, as he confesses in a later work, *The Treatise on Goldsmithing and Sculpture*, where he reveals that he destroyed many pages he had written about his patron "with much heart-burning and not without tears." This may be the reason that the *Autobiography* breaks off so abruptly.

This new edition of the *Autobiography* is intended to present Cellini the man as well as the age he describes. Contemporary works of art provide illustrations which have been integrated into the text. People, places and events are depicted by artists who were no less truthful with their brushes and chisels than Cellini was with his pen. Another dimension—the long perspective of history— is intended to combine with the text and the illustrations to enlarge the total experience.

Alfred Tamarin
New York, 1968

illustrations

viii

one

All men who have accomplished anything worthwhile should set down the story of their own lives with their own hands. But they should wait before undertaking so delicate an enterprise until they have passed the age of forty. This duty comes to my mind now that I am beyond fifty-eight, living in Florence, the city of my birth. I can remember many unpleasant things that happened to me, as they did to everyone else on this earth, but these troubles plague me less now than at any previous period of my career. Nay, it seems to me that I am more content in soul and body than ever before. I can recall many fortunes and some incredible misfortunes, which both frighten me and make me wonder how I ever reached this age of fifty-eight, wherein, thanks be to God, I am still going happily forward.

In a work like this there will always be times for natural bragging about many things, the first of which is for a man to let others know his worthy and ancient line-

Benvenuto Cellini, 1500–1571

age. I am called Benvenuto Cellini, son of Maestro Giovanni, son of Andrea, son of Cristofano Cellini. My mother was Madonna Elisabetta, daughter to Stefano Granacci. Both parents were citizens of Florence.

Old chronicles written by our ancestors reveal that the city of Florence was built in imitation of the fair city of Rome, with certain remnants of the Colosseum and Baths still to be traced near Santa Croce, the Capitol where is now the Old Market, and the entire Rotunda, still intact, originally made for Mars, now the Baptistry of San Giovanni. These were all built, they say, by Julius Caesar and some noble Romans, who undertook each to erect a notable edifice in this place. Among Julius Caesar's captains was a man of highest rank and valor, named Fiorino of Cellino. This Fiorino set up his quarters on the ground where Florence now stands so that he might be near the Arno River, causing all who had business with him to say, "Let us go to Fiorenze." Not only was his name Fiorino, which means "the flowered one," but the place he had chosen was rich with *fiore,* or flowers, which led Caesar to appoint the name Firenze, or Florence, to the city founded there.

Thus then we have learned, and thus we believe that we are descended from a man of worth. There are also Cellinis of our stock in Ravenna, an ancient town with many gentle folk. In Pisa are also some, and elsewhere in Christendom. Pisa breeds men of valor who are devoted to the profession of arms. I glory in tracing my descent from men of courage.

My ancestors, all men of notable bravery and devoted to arms, dwelt in Val d'Ambra, where they owned large estates and lived like little lords. In time, one son, Cristofano, roused a bitter feud with certain neighbors, as the result of which he was sent away to Florence. Cristofano married in Florence and had sons and daughters. One son was named Andrea, who came to be very well versed in

The valley of the River Arno, near Florence, by Leonardo da Vinci

architecture and lived by it as his trade. Andrea took a wife and had four sons, the third of whom was named Giovanni, who was afterward my father. My father paid more attention to architecture than any of his brothers and turned his mind also to music and good drawing, which are needed to practice the art of architecture well. He learned to play most excellently on the viol and the flute.

In the next house lived a man called Stefano Granacci, who had several daughters, all of them of remarkable beauty. As it pleased God, my father noticed one daughter named Elisabetta and asked for her in marriage. For eighteen years they enjoyed their wedded love, always desiring to be blessed with children. My mother miscarried of two boys, but later she gave birth to a girl, who was called Cosa. Two years later, my mother was once more with child. During her pregnancy she showed all those longings to which women in her condition are subject; they were exactly the same as during her former childbearing, so everyone made up his mind that another girl would be born. It happened that my mother gave birth on the night of All Saints, in the year 1500.

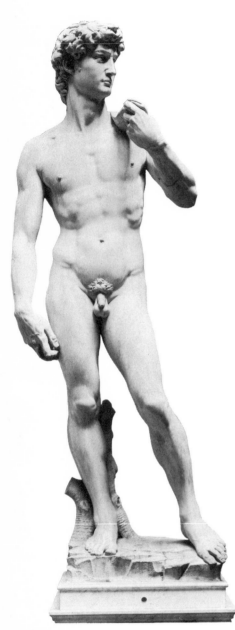

In Cellini's youth Florence was the center of the Renaissance. Michelangelo unveiled his David. Leonardo and Raphael were also at work in the city.

The midwife brought the baby to my father, Giovanni, and said, "I bring you a fine present, one you did not expect."

My father answered, in true philosophical fashion, that whatever God gave him would be dear to him. But when he saw the unexpected male child, he raised his eyes and said, "Lord, I thank Thee with my whole heart. This gift is very dear to me. Let him be welcome." Everyone asked him joyfully what name the child should bear. My father answered, "Let him be welcome—Benvenuto." And so it was resolved, and this name, Benvenuto, which means "welcome," was given to me at holy baptism, and by it I am still living with the grace of God.

My father began teaching me to play the flute and to sing by note. I was of that tender age when children enjoy whistles and such toys, nevertheless I had an inexpressible dislike for music, and played and sang only to be obedient. In those days my father made wonderful organs with pipes of wood, the best spinets that could then be seen, viols and lutes and harps of the most beautiful and perfect construction. He was an engineer and had marvelous skill in making machines for raising and lowering bridges, for working mills and other machinery of that sort. He was the first to fashion really well in ivory. But most of all he was devoted to his little flute, indeed, more than was proper. He was asked to become a member of the official city fifers of the Signory of Florence, which he did, neglecting thereby his fine engineering talent and his beautiful art. In those days the musicians of the Signory were all members of the most honorable trades, some belonging to the greatest guilds. That was why my father did not disdain to follow this profession and why his chief desire for me was that I should become a great performer on the flute. For my part, I was never more unhappy than when he talked about his dream for me, saying that he saw talent in me that could make me the best musician in the world.

4

Whenever my father spoke in this way about music, I begged him to let me spend a certain number of hours each day in sketching and drawing; I promised to give all the rest of my time to my music to satisfy him. My good father, driven to despair by this determination of mine, finally placed me in the workshop of Michel Agnolo, a master goldsmith, excellent in his craft, and father of that unworthy and dishonest Cavaliere Bandinelli, the sculptor, who was to become so great an antagonist of mine. After some days my father changed his mind and took me back, and, much to my discontent, I remained at music until I reached the age of fifteen. Then I returned to the goldsmith's trade, much against my father's will. I received no wages, which gave me freedom to indulge my whim for drawing as much as I desired. My liking for the art was so great or, I may truly say, my natural bent for it, that in a few months I caught up with the best young craftsmen in our business. To gratify my father I

When Cellini was twelve, Florentine independence ended; after the defeat of the republic's French allies Medici rule was restored through Cardinal Giovanni, who became Pope Leo X in 1514.

played on the flute or cornet from time to time. I even pretended to enjoy the music, too.

My younger brother, Cecchino, was a bold youth of fierce temper. He afterward became one of the chief soldiers of General Giovannino de' Medici, father of Duke Cosimo. Cecchino was fourteen, I two years older. One evening my brother was embroiled in a duel with a young man of twenty or thereabouts, in which I too became involved. As a consequence my brother and I were exiled for six months from Florence. We went to Siena, where a worthy man, who had befriended me in the past, gave me something to do, working at the goldsmith's trade.

We were recalled to Florence by the Cardinal de' Medici, who was to become Pope Clement VII. The Cardinal suggested to my father that I be sent to Bologna to learn more of the musician's art from a great master there. Delighted to be seeing the world, I went to Bologna cheerfully and stayed six months. Every day I went to my music lesson and made considerable progress, but I did even better as a goldsmith.

On another occasion I journeyed to Pisa, where I found work in my trade and soon was doing many things of beauty and importance. I spent my free hours and days diligently studying ancient objects and beautiful fragments of antiquity such as marble sarcophagi, and I made great progress in my art. All the time my father kept begging me to come home, and in every letter he implored me not to abandon the music he had taught me with so much trouble. On this, I suddenly gave up all desire to go back to him, and so much did I hate that accursed music that for the whole of my stay in Pisa, I never played the flute.

But at the end of the year I returned to Florence. About that time also a sculptor named Piero Torrigiano

A goldsmith's workshop: Cellini's apprenticeship began in 1515, the same year Francis I became king of France.

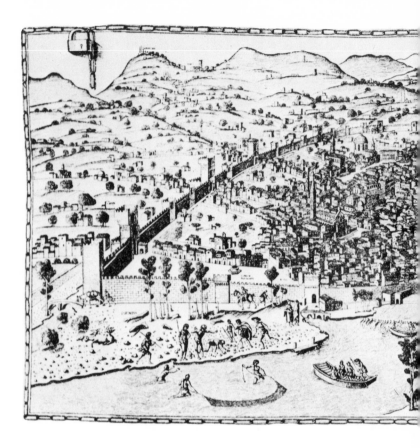

came to Florence from England. When he saw one of my drawings, he said to me, "I have undertaken a great work for King Henry VIII of England and want some of my own Florentines to help me. Your designs and method of working are worthier of a sculptor than a goldsmith. I have to turn out a great piece of bronze; at the same time I will turn you into a rich and able artist."

During this conversation, he noticed a copy I had done of Michelangelo Buonarroti's cartoon, which that divine master had made in competition with Leonardo da Vinci for the council hall in the palace of the Signory. This cartoon was the first masterpiece that had demonstrated the stupendous talents of Michelangelo. Both cartoons represented the taking of Pisa by the Florentines. Our admi-

Florence c. 1490

rable Leonardo had chosen to depict a battle of horses,
with the capture of some standards, in as divine a style
as could possibly be imagined. Michelangelo, in his cartoon, portrayed a number of foot soldiers, bathing in the
Arno. They are drawn at the moment of the sounding of
the alarm, all naked, running to arms. They are so splendid
in their action that nothing survives of ancient or modern
art which reaches the same lofty point of excellence. These
two cartoons stood, one in the palace of the Medici, the
other in the hall of the People. As long as they remained,
they were models which all the world studied and admired.
And though the divine Michelangelo in later life finished
the Sistine Chapel of Pope Julius, he never rose halfway to
the same pitch of power.

9

Meanwhile Piero Torrigiano, holding my drawing, told this story: "This Buonarroti and I used to go, as boys, into the Church of the Carmine to study the frescoes of Masaccio. It was Buonarroti's habit to banter with all who were drawing there. One day he annoyed me so much that I hit him on the nose with such a blow that I felt bone and cartilage crush under my knuckles. This mark of mine he will carry to the grave."

These words stirred such hatred in me, since I was always looking at Michelangelo's masterpieces, that even though I wanted to go to England with Torrigiano, I now could not bear the sight of him.

*A*ll the time that I was in Florence, I studied the noble manner of Michelangelo, and from this I have never deviated. About this time I made friends with an amiable lad

To immortalize Florence's independent spirit, Michelangelo and Leonardo created cartoons for a mural, the originals of which are now lost. But some of Leonardo's small sketches for his The Battle of Anghiari *still survive (facing page); also Peter Paul Rubens' drawing (below). An engraving and a drawing of a detail (both on facing page) suggest the power of Michelanglo's lost* The Battle of Cascina.

The Brancacci Chapel, Church of
the Carmine, where the sculptor
Torrigiano told Cellini he had
attacked the young Michelangelo;
(right) detail of Masaccio fresco

of my own age, also in the goldsmith's trade, who was
called Francesco. He was a son of Filippino Lippi and a
grandson of Fra Lippo Lippi, that most excellent painter. The
house where he lived was full of fine studies and drawings,
which his father had made of the best antiquities in Rome.
The sight of these things filled me with passionate enthu-

siasm. For two years or thereabouts we lived in intimacy. At this time I fashioned a silver bas-relief as big as a little child's hand, which was intended as a clasp for a man's belt. When it was exhibited, the goldsmiths praised me as the best young craftsman of their art.

One evening I was angry with my father for the same old reason of music, when I had a conversation with a wood carver, of my own age, named Il Tasso, about leaving Florence and going to Rome. He, too, was angry because of some disagreement with his mother. Thus talking, we found ourselves at the gate leading to Rome, whereupon I said, "Friend Tasso, this is God's doing; and now that I am at this gate, it seems to me that I have finished half the journey to Rome."

Michelangelo's portrait reveals a broken nose.

And so, being of one mind, we set out at once and walked almost in silence to Siena. There I hired a horse, and the good Tasso and I, singing and laughing, traveled the whole way to Rome. I was just nineteen years old and so was the century.

In Rome I put myself for a while under a master, for whom I worked on a fine piece of silver plate for a cardinal. I enriched it with many elegant designs of my own, and my master boasted that so good a piece of work had been turned out from his shop. It was so constructed as to serve as a saltcellar at the table.

At the end of two years I returned to Florence and once more put myself to work under many masters. I worked with many different persons, some worthy men, but also others who robbed me grossly. The bad men among my masters were called Salvadore and Michele Guasconti. So I left their company and took part of a goldsmithing shop which stood at the side of the New Market. There I finished several pretty pieces, which aroused the jealousy of the Guascontis, who had three big shops and carried on a thriving trade.

One day, near the shop of one of the Guascontis, a cousin of that family, Gherardo by name, started a fight with me, whereupon I struck him such a blow that he fell

stunned. His family rushed to the governors of Florence, who were called the Eight, and falsely charged me with assaulting them in their shops, sword in hand, a thing unheard of in Florence. The magistrates had me summoned and seriously considered sending me to prison. My adversaries had talked with the magistrates in private, but I, innocent in such matters, had trusted in the justice of my cause. Finally I was sentenced to pay four measures of flour to a nunnery.

I was so angry that I dashed out of the palace when the guard was not watching, ran to my shop, seized my dagger and rushed to the house of my enemies, who were together at table. Storming with rage, I attacked Gherardo. I fought off twelve others of the household, who were armed with an iron shovel, a thick iron pipe, an anvil, hammers and cudgels. In the melee I only lost my cap. After the fracas was over, it was found that not a single man had been injured.

But I ran off and found sanctuary in the cell of a good friar, who assured me of safety. The governors of Florence, in an extraordinary meeting, pronounced a most dreadful ban against me and against anyone offering me protection. My father brought me a suit of armor and a fine sword. With 10 golden crowns I escaped from the city disguised as a monk. I went by night to Siena on horseback, where I joined the mail carriers headed for Rome. On the way, we heard news of the new Pope, Clement VII.

Raphael's portrait of the worldly Medicis: Pope Leo X and, left, Cardinal Giulio, who became Pope Clement VII

ROME

Urbis Romae, totius olim orbis domitricis, situs: cum adhuc extantibus, sacrosanctae vetustatis monumentis

PIRRHO LIGORIO NEAP.
INVENTOR

AED · AVG ·
CASTRVM PRAE TORIVM

VIVARIVM

PORTA clausa

VIA TIBVRTINA
Porte S. Laurent
Porta S. Laurentij
Gallus
T. MINERVA
T. de Mire

S. Agnetis
PORT. NVMENTANA

BACCHI
Le Temple de Bacus

PORT. SALARIA

PORT. PINCIANA

Les Sepulcres de Neron et de Domitian

Place de Saluste

HIPPODROMVS
HORT. SALVSTIANI
FOR. SALVSTII

GESTATIO ALEXAN. AVG
S. Eusebe — S. Eusebij
AGGERES TARQVINII SVPERBI

THERMAE DIOCLETIANI

S. Marie Maior
Basilica S. Maria Maiori

S. Potentiana

VIMINALIS

SEPVLCHR. NERONIS VEL DOMITII

Temple de la Trinité
T. TRINITATIS
T. Fortu T. de la Fortune

COLLIS HORTVLORVM

Maison de Vespasian
DOMVS VESPASIANI
MALVM PVNICVM
S. Laurentij in Paliperna

V. de Grimani
Alta Semita
THE. CONSTANTINI

CIR. FLORAL.

V. de Ferrara

QVIRINALIS

Ther. Constantini

FALLIS SVBVRRA

S. Petri in Vincula
FORVM NERVE

NAVMACHIE
SEPTA

ACQVA

S. Marie du Peuple
S. MARIA DE POPVLO

VIA FLAMINIA

P. Popolo p. peuple

M. ACITORIVS

FORVM Augusti
Colonne Traiane
Superficie Fori Augusti
FORVM Traiani
Foro Traiani

Adrian
VIA SACRA
FORVM CVRIAE
VELIA
PALATIN
GERMALVS

DOMVS TITI AVG
T. Paris T. Lunret Soleil
CARINAE
CVRIA Vetus
VICVS

Minerva T. AGRIPP
PANTHEON
CAM. MARTII

CAPITOLIVM Le Capitolle
Palatium Conservatoru

FORV BOARIV
IANI

CIRC. AGONALIS
VILLA Medici
Campus flore

THEAT. MARCELL
PISCARIA

SCH. GRAECA FOR. OLITO
ST. LVCERIVM

le Jardin de Domitian
HORT. DOMI TIAE
MOLES ADRIANI
Chasteau S. Ange
Castel S. Angelo

CIRCVS NERONIS

PORTA CASTELLI
La porte du Chasteau

La Porte du Pallais
PORTA PALATII

BELVEDERE

Piazza de San Pietro
BASIL. S. PETRI

PORTA TORRIONIS

Obelisco
VATICANVS

S. honofre

HORT. MARTALA MICVS

S. PETRI in Monte

S. MARIA

Pont S. spiritus
Porte des S. spirit

two

In Rome I found work in the shop of a master goldsmith
and began to make some candelabra for the Bishop of
Salamanca, a Spaniard. The candelabra were richly chased,
so far as that sort of work allows.

During this time I often went to sketch, sometimes in
Michelangelo's Sistine Chapel, and sometimes in the house
of Agostino Chigi of Siena, which contained many incomparable paintings by that great master Raphael. One day I
was making a copy of a Jove by Raphael when the lady
of the house and her friend Madonna Porzia spoke to me.
Both were women of great beauty. When I told them that
I was a goldsmith, I was immediately asked to design an
ornament, and then commissioned to finish it, which I did
in twelve days in the form of a fleur-de-lis, decorated with
little masks, children and animals, exquisitely enameled.
The diamonds which formed the lily were set off so that
they seemed doubled in beauty.

Meanwhile I contrived to get an order from the Bishop
of Salamanca for one of those great water vessels which
are used for ornaments on sideboards. I set my hand with

17

Cellini's jewel for Madonna Porzia was patterned after the Farnese family emblem.

marvelous good will to this piece of plate. At that time a musician in the Pope's band sent word to inquire whether I was inclined to help them at the Pope's Ferragosto, the feast of August, playing my soprano cornet in some motets of great beauty. Although I had the greatest desire to finish the vase, yet, because I wished to please my old father, I consented to join them.

On the first of August, while Pope Clement was at table, we played those motets so well that his Holiness protested that he had never heard music more sweetly performed. The Pope expressed his wish to have me in his service with the other bandsmen. I meditated whether I ought to accept, inasmuch as I could not but suffer if I neglected the noble studies of my art. The following night my father appeared to me in a dream and begged me, for God's love and his, to enter upon this engagement, threatening me with a father's curse if I did not. When I woke, I ran, for very fright, to have myself enrolled in the Pope's service. Then I wrote to my old father, telling him the news. In his answer, he told me that he too had dreamed nearly the same as I had.

I set myself with indefatigable industry to the completion of the vase I had begun for the Bishop of Salamanca. That prelate was a very extraordinary man, extremely rich, but difficult to please. He sent daily to learn what I was doing. When his messenger did not find me at home, he broke into fury, saying that he would give the work to others to finish. This was the result of my slavery to that accursed music. Still I labored diligently night and day until I brought my work to a point when it could be exhibited. I submitted it to the Bishop, which so increased his desire to see it finished that I was sorry I had shown it. At the end of three months I had it ready, with little animals and foliage and masks, as beautiful as one could hope to see. Lifting up the vase, the Bishop cried like a true Spaniard, "I swear by God that I will take as long in paying him as

Galatea *by Raphael, still in the Villa Farnesina, where Cellini was sketching when he met Madonna Porzia*

Detail of Michelangelo's ceiling for the Sistine Chapel, completed only eleven years before Cellini came to Rome

he has lagged in making it." When I heard this, I was exceedingly put out, and fell to cursing all Spain and everyone who wished it well.

Among other beautiful ornaments, this vase had a handle with a most delicate spring mechanism. One day a certain Spanish gentleman worked the handle too roughly and the gentle spring broke in his hand. The grandee begged the butler who was in charge of the Bishop's silver to take the vase quickly to the master who had made it and have it mended at once. So the vase came once more into my hands. I promised to put it in order forthwith, which indeed I did.

Soon the man who had brought the vase came running back, all in a sweat, and demanded it, crying that the Monsignor wanted to show it to certain other gentlemen. But I did not mean to be so quick. The serving man flew into such a rage that he reached for his sword and threatened to wreck my entire shop. I put a stop to this with my own weapon. I told him quite spiritedly, "I am not going to give it to you! Go and tell Monsignor, your master, that I want the money for my work before I let it leave this shop." The fellow begged and pleaded, promising to see to it that I should be paid. At last he swore he would come back with Spaniards enough to cut me to pieces.

I resolved that I would defend myself with courage. So I got an admirable little gun ready, which I used for shooting game. A crowd of Spaniards arrived, led by their major-domo, who bade them break into my shop, take the vase and give me a good beating. Hearing these words, I showed them the muzzle of my gun and prepared to fire, threatening to blow out all their brains. I turned the muzzle toward the major-domo and made as though to discharge it. He clapped spurs to the small horse he was riding and fled headlong. The Spaniards were compelled to relate the whole affair to the Bishop, who upbraided his men because they had undertaken such an act of violence. He was also angry that, having begun, they had not gone through with it.

A pitcher in the manner of Cellini

Renaissance artists were inspired by the rediscovery of classical Rome: ruins of the ancient Forum c. 1532–35.

The Bishop sent word that if I did not bring the vase at once, he would make mincemeat of me; but if I brought it, he would pay its full price. These threats were so far from terrifying me that I answered that I was going immediately to lay my case before the Pope. Pope Clement heard the story and spoke warmly in praise of me and my vase. Bishop Salamanca repented and offered me large commissions, but I replied that I would have to be paid in advance, which made the Pope laugh heartily.

I did much work for the palace and executed many commissions for many cardinals, so that I earned plenty of

money. Madonna Porzia advised me to open a shop, which I did. I never stopped working for that excellent and gentle lady, who paid me exceedingly well, and by whose means, perhaps, I came to make a figure in the world.

At that time, while I was still a young man of about twenty-three, there raged a plague of such extraordinary violence that many thousands died of it every day in Rome. I had formed a habit of going on feast days to the ancient buildings and copying parts of them in wax or with the pencil. These buildings are all ruins and attract innumerable pigeons, so it came into my head to use my gun against these birds. Avoiding all contact with people, in my terror of the plague, I used to take a fowling piece and oftentimes came home laden with the fattest pigeons. I did not charge my gun with more than a single ball; and thus it was by pure skill that I filled heavy bags. I had a fowling piece which I had made myself. I also used to make a very fine powder, in doing which I discovered secret processes, beyond any known at that time. When I loaded my gun with powder weighing one-fifth of the ball, it carried two hundred paces point-blank, which will astonish good shots of every degree. My natural temperament was melancholy, so this kind of amusement made my heart leap up with joy. I found I could work better and with far greater mastery than when I spent all my time only in study and manual labor.

The whole world was now at war. The Constable of Bourbon, learning that there were no armed troops in Rome, pushed his army with utmost energy up to the city. Bourbon's army arrived before the walls of Rome and I went to look the scene over. I could see that famous army, making every effort to gain entrance to the town. The battle was raging desperately. Several of our defenders lay dead upon the ramparts, slain by the besiegers. I aimed my arquebus where I saw the thickest ranks of fighting men and fired it at a figure that seemed higher than all the rest.

22

*Castle St. Angelo, 1514–15,
and the route Clement VII would
take for refuge from the army of
Charles V*

Soon the enemy was in the most extraordinary confusion.
Afterward I learned that one of our shots had killed the
Constable of Bourbon, and from what I subsequently discovered, he was the man whom I had first noticed above
the heads of the rest.

Leaving the ramparts, I reached the castle of St.
Angelo, where, against my will, I was forced to join forces
with the papal household. I went up to the tower and
came upon certain pieces of artillery which were not being
used properly enough to do any real damage to the enemy.
I took over the firing matches, aimed some of the guns at

23

points where I saw it would be useful and killed with them a good number of the enemy. Had it not been for this, the troops who poured into Rome that morning and were marching straight upon the castle might possibly have entered it with ease. I went on firing under the eyes of several cardinals and lords, who kept blessing me and giving me their heartiest encouragement. Let it suffice that it was I who saved the castle that morning.

That evening Pope Clement appointed a great Roman nobleman to be captain of all the gunners. He greeted me with utmost kindness and stationed me with five fine pieces of artillery on the highest point of the castle, to

The Constable of Bourbon, commanding the army of Charles V, was shot dead before the walls of Rome, but it is not certain that Cellini's bullet was responsible. The army burned and looted the Eternal City in what is known as The Sack of Rome.

which the name of the Angel specially belongs. This circular eminence goes round the castle and looks out over the town of Rome. The captain put under my orders enough men to manage my guns and begged me to keep on as I had begun. I was perhaps more inclined by nature to the profession of arms than to the one I had adopted and I took great pleasure in it. Night came, the enemy had entered Rome and we, in the castle, looked down on unbelievable scenes of tumult and fire in the streets below. We were beleaguered in the castle for a whole month, during which I never missed my artillery practice.

One day the captain of artillery had me come down

Pope Clement VII besieged in the Castle St. Angelo because he had shifted his alliance to France. The city of Florence took advantage of Pope Clement's imprisonment to expel the Medicis again.

from the tower to fire on some house nearby, where certain of our besiegers were meeting. An enemy cannon shot hit a battlement near me, and the debris struck me in the chest and took my breath away. I lay stretched on the ground like a dead man, surrounded by great uproar and lamentation. One of my comrades ran up and put a potion of wormwood and hot Greek wine on my breast, which immediately restored my scattered faculties. I tried to speak but could not, for some stupid soldiers had filled my mouth with earth, imagining that they were giving me the sacrament.

From time to time some of the cardinals who lived in the castle came to watch me. I often told them not to show themselves since their nasty red caps were conspicuous targets for our enemies. Finally I had them barred, and thus gained their deep ill will. On one occasion the shock of the blast of my gun dislodged a barrel full of stones, which almost felled Cardinal Farnese, who afterward became Pope Paul III. Of Farnese I shall say nothing more, because it will appear in its proper place how well it would have been if I had killed him. On another day, Pope Clement, walking round the circular keep, saw me make a direct hit on a Spanish colonel who had formerly been in his service. The Pope sent for me, and I explained all the devices I had used in firing. Upon bended knee I besought him to give me the pardon of his blessing for that homicide, and for all the others I had committed in the service of the Church. The Pope blessed me and gave me pardon. But my drawing and my fine studies in my craft and my charming art of music, all were swallowed up in the din of that artillery.

Papal tiaras were masterpieces of the jeweler's art.

Pope Clement, wishing to save the Pope's crowns as well as the whole papal collection of great jewels, ordered me to take the gems out of their gold settings, which I did. I wrapped them separately in pieces of paper and sewed them into the linings of the Pope's clothes. Then I was given all the gold, which weighed about two hundred pounds, to melt down as secretly as I could. I had my lodging then in the tower, where I could lock the door and be free of interruption. I built a little draft furnace of bricks and threw the gold upon the coals, where it gradually sank through and dropped into a pan. While I was engaged in this, I still kept up constant barrages from my artillery pieces, inflicting considerable damage on the enemy in their trenches less than a stone's throw below us.

One evening, a little before vespers, I noticed some one of the enemy, riding along the margin of a trench on muleback. The mule was trotting very quickly, and the man was talking to the soldiers in the trenches. Taking careful aim at him, I hit the mark. A fragment of my missile struck the man in the face and the rest struck the mule, which fell dead. A tremendous uproar rose from the enemy trench. The man turned out to be the Prince of Orange, who was carried to a certain tavern in the neighborhood, where in a short while all the chieftains of the besieging army gathered together.

Pope Clement summoned me and inquired about the event. Then, with shrewd instinct, he ordered all bombardiers to train their artillery at the tavern and to fire simultaneously on a given signal. He judged that if we killed the generals, the army, already almost on the point of breaking up, would take to flight. But one cardinal protested, saying that they were at the point of concluding an agreement with the attackers. Our orders were countermanded. But I, chafing at the leash, let blaze one of my demi-cannons just before the order to hold my fire reached me. This shot did much damage to the enemy. The cardinal would gladly have had me hanged or put to death, but the Pope defended me with spirit.

After I melted down all the gold, I took it to the Pope, who ordered me given 25 crowns for my pains, apologizing to me for his inability to give me more.

A few days afterward the articles of peace were signed.

three

I left Rome, wanting to see my father and to lift the ban which was still in force against me. When I reached home, I found my good father, who thought that either I had been killed in the sack of Rome or that I would come back a beggar. I did neither, for I was alive, with plenty of money, a fellow to wait on me, and a good horse. My joy on greeting the old man was so intense that, while he embraced and kissed me, I thought I must die on the spot. I gave him a good quantity of crowns which I had earned by my soldiering, and he left to buy off my banishment. But when he learned that I might soon again be required to do military service in Florence, the poor old man was greatly disturbed. He had one son, he exclaimed, who was already a most valiant soldier, and I ought not abandon the noble arts, in which I had labored so many years with such diligence. Then he said to me, "Oh, my dear son, the plague in this town is raging with unceasing violence, and I am always afraid you will come home infected with it. I pray and command you, for the love of me, pack off and go to

Mantua; and I would rather you do this today, not tomorrow."

I had always taken pleasure in seeing the world, and never having been in Mantua, I went there very willingly. There I visited Messer Giulio Romano, that most excellent painter, who was living like a lord and executing a great work for the Duke in a place called Del Te. Messer Giulio brought me to the Duke, who wanted me to make a model for a shrine to hold the blood of Christ, which they have there in Mantua. The Cardinal, the Duke's brother, wanted me to make the pontifical seal of his most reverend Lordship, which I finished after four months, together with several other little pieces for the Duke. But while I was working, I came down with a fever, during which, in delirium, I cursed Mantua and its master. These words, reported to the Duke, made him fly into a passion against me. Since I was out of temper with Mantua, our bad feelings were reciprocal.

I left Mantua and arrived back in Florence, hoping to find my dear father, but he and all the people in the house had died of the plague, except only my sister, Liperata. I received news also that my brother was alive. Our joy at embracing one another was extravagant.

On the entreaty of my brother and sister, I remained now for some time in Florence and worked on some golden medals which interested Michelangelo Buonarroti. The divine master gave such praises to my work that I felt incredibly inspired to further effort. He even sketched a design for a gold medal, showing Atlas bearing the world on his shoulders, for a young man of lofty spirit, named Frederigo Ginori. I also made a model in wax, which was very different from Michelangelo's. When Michelangelo saw it, he praised me to the skies.

Not long thereafter Frederigo Ginori died, and the Atlas came into the hands of another, who afterward gave it to Francis, the king of France. His Majesty, exceedingly delighted with the gift, expressed a wish to know me.

During Pope Clement's difficulties with the city of

The plague and its aftermath of starvation and death; fourteenth century fresco (facing page)

Florence, a militia was organized in each quarter of the town and I received orders to serve my turn. I provided myself with a rich outfit and went about with the highest nobility. Letters from Rome, however, informed me that his Holiness was asking for me and suggested also that I ought not to stand against a Pope in a party of such harebrained radicals. I was thrown into such a fright that I hastened to entrust my affairs to a friend and to rush back to Rome.

There I went to see the Pope, who was in bed, suffering from a slight indisposition. When he set eyes on me, he was exceedingly glad. I kissed his feet and said, "Most blessed Father, from the time of the sack of Rome up to this hour I have been unable to go to confession, because

I have been refused absolution. The reason is this: When I melted down the gold, your Holiness ordered that a modest reward be given to me, but I actually received nothing. When the gold was melted, however, I found a pound and a half of tiny grains, which I kept, intending to give back its worth as soon as I could. I beg you, grant me forgiveness so that I can confess and regain the grace of my Lord God."

The Pope, with a scarcely perceptible sigh, said, "I am very sorry that your reward was so little, but I make you a present of whatever sum you say it was. In addition, I give you my full pardon."

On another occasion his Holiness told me that if I had come to Rome sooner, I would have been commissioned to

Reconciled with the Pope, Emperor Charles V put down Florentine insurgency in 1530 and restored Medici rule in the person of the twenty-year-old Alessandro. It was this siege of Florence that Cellini abandoned at the Pope's command.

restore the two tiaras which had been pulled to pieces in the castle. "Instead," the Pope said, "I will employ you on a piece of the very greatest importance, a button for my cope. It is to be as big as a trencher. Upon it I want you to represent a God the Father, in half relief, and in the middle to set a magnificent big diamond and several other gems of the greatest value. I want it to be finished quickly so that I may enjoy the use of it for a little while."

I pushed ahead on my model for the Pope's button with all diligence. There was considerable jealousy among certain goldsmiths who thought themselves more capable of doing the piece. They made designs, but the Pope would not look at them until I had completed my model. One morning I brought the model to the Pope. My rivals came rushing up with their designs. The Pope examined the designs and then my model and cried his enthusiastic approval of the dexterous device I had employed for combining the diamond with the figure of God the Father. I was in the utmost impatience to begin work. Eight days later the Pope summoned me. He wanted to see what I was doing and I showed him the golden plate on which I had carved the figure of God the Father. The Pope examined it with astonishment and pleasure. Then he told me that he wished me also to make dies for the coinage of his realm. He ordered me to make a model for a gold doubloon, upon which he wanted a naked Christ. On the reverse were to be a Pope and an emperor propping up a falling cross.

Cellini's button for Clement VII

Quickly I made two dies of steel and stamped a coin in gold. The Pope was greatly gratified at the work and the speed with which I performed it. I took the opportunity to ask him for the post of stamp master in the Mint, a place worth 6 golden crowns a month, in addition to the dies which were paid for at the rate of a ducat for three.

At this period my brother was also in Rome, serving Duke Alessandro, who esteemed him highly as the bravest soldier in his service. One day an old comrade of my brother's was being taken to prison and a fight started in the street in which my brother's dearest friend was reported killed. Trying to avenge his friend, my brother was hit by a bullet above the knee of his right leg. I came upon Cecchino, lying stretched upon the ground, but did not recognize him. Accordingly he called out, "Dearest brother, do not be upset by my accident. It is only what might be expected in my profession. Get me moved from here at once, for I have but a few hours to live."

I comforted him and vowed that I would avenge him on the spot, but I was held back. The doctors, who were called, could not save him. He lost blood copiously, for nothing could be done to stop the flow. All the following night he was off his head, raving deliriously and pouring forth a torrent of terrible frenzies and curses. When the sun appeared above the horizon, he turned to me, and kicking his feet as though flinging himself across a horse's back, he called out, "Farewell, farewell!" and with these words that most valiant spirit passed away.

At the proper hour, toward nightfall, I had him buried with due ceremony in the church of the Florentines. Afterward I erected to his memory a handsome monument of marble carved with trophies and banners. My brother was twenty-five years old. He was nicknamed Cecchino del Piffero, the fifer's son. His real name was Giovanfrancesco Cellini.

I kept working on the gold button for Pope Clement and on the dies for the Mint, even though I was plunged in great grief over the loss of my brother. My work was

Cellini: gold coins for Clement VII

affected badly. Day and night I kept watching the rifleman who had shot Cecchino. Finally I decided I had to get rid of my torment, so one evening I stole up on him and dealt him a backhanded stroke with which I meant to cut his head clean off. But he turned suddenly and the blow fell upon his shoulder. He fled, but I followed after him and plunged my dagger into his neck so deeply that, though I used all my strength, I could not pull it out. Just at that moment, four soldiers, with swords drawn, sprang out against me and I made off, fearing that I might be recognized.

For eight days the Pope did not send for me. When he summoned me, I was made to understand that his Holiness knew all about the affair, but as he was well inclined toward me, I had only to mind my work and keep quiet. The Pope looked me straight in the face and said, "Now that you are cured, Benvenuto, take heed how you live!"

Understanding his meaning, I promised that I would. I immediately opened a very fine shop, and there I finished the jewel in a few months.

While I was working on the Pope's button, as well as for the Mint, certain pieces of false money got abroad in Rome, stamped with my dies. Suspicion was directed against me, even by the Pope, but I showed him that I could make more profit for myself by my art than by counterfeiting coins, which satisfied him. Soon a stamper and a metalworker, both employed in the Mint, were found to be the guilty rogues. One was hanged and the other sent to the galleys.

When I finished my piece for the Pope, it was held to be the finest masterpiece which had ever been seen in Rome. The Pope was insatiable in praising me and offering me rewards. I begged his Holiness for a small favor, a macebearer's post which happened to be vacant. The Pope said he had in mind to grant me something of far greater consequence, but I pleaded for the post as a pledge, which was accordingly done. It brought me in a little less than 200 crowns a year.

Sebastiano del Piombo: portrait of Clement VII

I continued to work for the Pope, and he commissioned me to execute a chalice of exceeding richness. I designed it with three fair-sized figures in the round, representing Faith, Hope and Charity, and with three stories in low relief at the base of the cup. One story was the Nativity of Christ, the second, the Resurrection and the third, St.

Peter crucified, head downward.

While I was at this work, I asked the Pope for a post in the Piombo, the Office of Seals, which had come vacant. The Pope, forgetting his former promises, seemed reluctant to give it to me. This set me off in a huge fury against the Pope, which I expressed openly. When I left, the painter Sebastian of Venice requested the post. The Pope replied, "That devil Benvenuto will not accept a rebuke. I meant to give him the post but it is not right for anyone to be so haughty with a Pope."

Thus he let it be known to me that I had obtained the office for the painter Sebastian, who came to be known as Sebastian del Piombo.

My work on the chalice did not proceed as quickly as I could have wished. The Pope gave me no gold to complete the piece. At the same time I suffered an attack of inflammation in the eyes, so serious that I expected to be left without my eyesight. It happened also that a Milanese goldsmith, Tobbia by name, was brought to Rome, and we were each commissioned to furnish a design for mounting a unicorn's horn in a setting of gold, which was to be a gift for King Francis. My design, no sooner was it seen, made everyone decide in its favor, but certain gentlemen of consequence prevailed on the Pope, arguing that the French court was not cultivated enough to understand the excellence of my work, and further, that I should devote myself to completing the chalice, which the Pope was anxious to obtain. Thus Tobbia was commissioned to mount the unicorn's horn and I was bidden to finish the cup. I replied that I desired nothing in the world more than to complete the work, but since it was to be made of gold his Holiness must provide me with some of the precious metal.

All I had spoken was reported to the Pope, who flew into a passion and swore he would not believe that I was so mad as not to finish the work. More than two months passed in this fashion. I declared I would not lift a finger on the cup, but actually I kept working on it with the greatest diligence. The Pope began to show real displeasure with me and declared publicly he would punish me in one way or another. Another jeweler from Milan in the papal service, called Pompeo, was present when these words were spoken. He was closely related to Messer Traiano, a favored servant of Pope Clement. The Pope, being angry with me, was persuaded by the two men to take away my post at the Mint. Pompeo came to inform me that I had been deprived of the Mint and threatened that I would lose other things besides if I did not finish the chalice. I retorted angrily that his Holiness was hurting himself, not me, by taking away the Mint. I burst out that nothing would induce me to accept the post again, even if the Pope changed his mind and wanted to give it back.

Eight days later the Pope sent Pompeo to tell me that he wanted the chalice exactly as it was, saying that he did not intend for me to finish it. I told Pompeo, "This thing is not like the Mint, which it was in his Holiness' power to take away. Only five hundred crowns which I had received belonged to his Holiness, and I am ready to return them. The piece itself is mine, and I shall do with it what I think best."

Three days later two papal chamberlains arrived. "The Pope has sent us, Benvenuto," they said. "Since you have chosen not to comply with his request on easy terms, his commands now are that either you give us his piece or we take you to prison."

I looked them cheerfully in the face and replied, "My lords, if I were to give the work to his Holiness, I should be giving what is mine and not his. At this moment I have no intention of making him a gift. I have brought it forward with great labor and do not want it to fall into the hands of some ignorant beast of a jeweler who will destroy it."

The two gentlemen put me between them and brought me to the Governor of Rome. He came at me, partly bullying, partly expostulating, partly giving advice, saying that it was only reasonable that a man who ordered work from another should be able to withdraw it at his choice.

In my defense I replied, "Nobody can command me further than that I should return the five hundred crowns which I have been paid. Go and tell the Pope that his threats do not frighten me, for I am an honest man and stand in no fear for my sins."

The Governor finally went to the Pope to find out his orders. For three hours I walked up and down a large hall before he returned. The word from the Pope was that I must bring my work to the Governor, who was to put it into a box, seal it and then take it to the Pope, who pledged his word not to break the seal and to return the piece untouched. This much he wanted done to preserve his own honor.

Accordingly, I sent for the piece and had it sealed. The Governor repaired again to the Pope, who turned the box this way and that several times and then, with some show of anger, removed the strings and seals with which it was done up. Much praise was bestowed on the work. It was shown to the goldsmith Tobbia who was asked if he thought he could finish the piece. When Tobbia said he could, the Pope told the Governor to try persuading me to give up the piece, or to set a definite time if I were bent on finishing it myself. Or, if he could persuade me in neither, he was to order me to take the 500 crowns to the Pope's jeweler Pompeo.

I took my piece and on the instant returned the 500 crowns to Pompeo. It is most likely that the Pope had

Cellini's medal of Clement VII (left), made to regain the Pope's lost favor; (middle) reverse, original design by Cellini; (right) alternate reverse, design suggested by Pope Clement VII

counted on some shortage of money preventing me from immediately putting my hands on so considerable a sum and was anxious in this way to mend the broken thread of my obedience.

The Pope thereafter sent word with that same Pompeo that I must not neglect the piece which would be used for a shrine to hold the Corpus Domini when the Pope walked in procession. I sent word that the greatest treasure I could wish would be to regain the favor of so great a Pope. I also warned Pompeo not to meddle with the least of my affairs or I would make him recognize his errors by the punishment they deserved. At that time I had begun to make a portrait of the Pope and was executing a medal in secret. On the reverse it had a figure of Peace, a slender woman dressed in very thin drapery, gathered at the waist, with a little torch in her hand which was burning a heap of arms bound like a trophy. In the background I had shown part of a temple, to which Discord was fettered.

On a day in April, the weather very fair, I brought the medal and the dies of steel to the Pope, who recognized at once the mastery of art and said, "The ancients never had such medals as these." His Holiness then told me he would like another design on the reverse of the medal, according to a fancy of his own. He commissioned me to design the story of Moses when he strikes the rock and water gushes from it. "Benvenuto," he added, "you will not have finished it before I have provided for your future."

So I devoted myself entirely to working out this reverse with the Moses on it. When it was completed, I took it to the Pope, whom I found in bed in a most deplorable condition. Three days later he died, and I was left with my labor lost.

four

In the great commotion which always happens on such occasions, as the death of a Pope, my quarrel with Pompeo came to a head. I was sitting in the street with several friends, when Pompeo, attended by ten very well-armed men, walked by and taunted me derisively. I forbore, knowing that if I drew my sword, terrible mischief might result for innocent persons. Instead I followed Pompeo and his braves to an apothecary shop, where, I learned, he boasted of the insult he thought he had put upon me. When he came out, he was immediately surrounded by his henchmen. I drew a little dagger and broke through the line of his defenders so quickly and coolly that none was able to prevent me. I aimed to strike Pompeo in the face, but he turned his head in fright and I stabbed him just beneath the ear. I only gave two blows, for he fell stone dead at the second. I had not meant to kill him, but as the saying goes, knocks are not dealt by measure. I drew my sword to defend myself, but those brave souls took no action against me. So I went back alone, considering how best to restore myself to safety. Most of the young men

Cellini: gold coins for Paul III

around agreed that Pompeo had done me too great and unforgivable an injury. They marveled that I had put up with him so long.

Cardinal Cornaro, on hearing of the affair, sent to bring me to his quarters. The Cardinal de' Medici also offered to be my protector.

A few days afterward Cardinal Farnese was elected Pope Paul III. The new Pope sent for me, saying that he did not wish anyone else to strike his coins. When he was informed that I was in hiding for the murder of Pompeo, he ordered a safe conduct to be made out for me, and I began at once to serve him. I was treated with the utmost favor. I took the dies in hand, designing a St. Paul, which gave more satisfaction than the models of my competitors. I had it in my heart to recover the post of stamper at the Mint, but the Pope thought that first I must obtain pardon for killing Pompeo, and this pardon I should get on St. Mary's holy day in August in Rome. It is usual on this solemn festival to grant freedom to twelve outlaws. Meanwhile he promised me another safe conduct which should keep me safely until that time.

My enemies, however, resorted to another trick. The slain Pompeo had left 3000 ducats as a dowry for his illegitimate daughter. It was contrived that a certain country lad, a favorite of the Pope's son, Signor Pier Luigi, should get her hand in marriage. The groom got little of the dowry, since his lordship had a mind to use it himself. To please his wife, the new husband begged the prince to have me arrested. This the Pope's son promised to do as soon as the first flush of my favor with the Pope had died away.

I had an inkling of these schemes, yet I did not neglect to present myself to Signor Pier Luigi, who made a pretense of treating me with great distinction. He had, however, decided to do one or the other of two things—either to have me assassinated or to have me imprisoned by the Sheriff, or Bargello, as he is called. Accordingly he commissioned a certain little devil of a Corsican soldier in his service to do away with me as cleverly as possible. Seeing into their plot, I went about with my eyes open, wearing an undercoat and armlets of chain mail. One day, after dinner, the Corsican devil and I met in the middle of the road. Folks gathered quickly around us, for it became clear that we meant swords and daggers. But the little devil did not have the spirit to lay hands on me.

Not many days later, I learned that Signor Pier Luigi had given strict orders that I be arrested that very evening. I spoke with some of my friends, who advised me to be off at once, and accordingly I left with the post for Florence.

In Florence Duke Alessandro gave me orders at once to strike dies for his coinage, the first a piece of 40 soldi with the Duke's head on one side. This was in silver, and it gave so much satisfaction that the Duke did not hesitate to say these were the best pieces of money in Christendom. All Florence agreed, and so did everyone else who saw

Pier Luigi Farnese, son of Pope Paul III; Titian's portrait hints at his darker side.

*Duke Alessandro de' Medici, misshapen, profligate and violent
—first hereditary duke of Florence*

them. I struck four other sorts of coins to the satisfaction of the Duke.

His Excellency next told me to execute a die of his portrait, which I began in wax. The Duke gave orders to admit me whenever I needed him to sit for the portrait. Oftentimes I found him napping after dinner with that Lorenzino of his, who afterward murdered him. At that time I received from Rome a full safe conduct from the Pope, with advice to go there at once and get the pardon of Our Lady's feast in mid-August in order to clear myself from my crime of homicide. I went immediately to the Duke, and having finished the waxen medal, showed him the safe conduct and told him how his Holiness had recalled me to execute certain pieces of work. I soon took my leave and left the Duke and Lorenzino alone together.

On the day following my return to Rome, I went to my little dwelling, which my partner, Felice, had put in excellent order. That night, more than an hour before daybreak, I heard a furious pounding at the door and made my servant see who the madman was who knocked so brutally at that hour. I made haste to put an excellent coat of mail over my shirt and, over that, some clothes which I caught up at random. My servant returned, exclaiming, "Heavens, master, it is the Sheriff and all his guard. He says if you do not open at once, he will knock the door down!"

Supposing it was a trap laid to murder me, I seized an excellent dagger with my right hand and with my left I took the safe conduct. The Bargello and the officers sprang inside, thinking they could easily lay hands on me. But when they saw me prepared to receive them, they fell back. I threw my safe conduct to them and said, "Read that! And since you cannot seize me, I do not mean that you shall touch me!"

The Bargello ordered some men to arrest me, saying he would look at my safe conduct later. I presented my arms boldly, calling aloud, "Let God defend the right! Either I shall escape alive or be taken dead!" The Bargello

Cellini: silver coin portrait of Duke Alessandro; reverse, San Cosimo and San Damiano

The sack of Tunis

saw he could not take me except as I had said. Accordingly he had the safe conduct read and threw it on the ground. They went away without their prize.

Meanwhile the feast of Our Lady came around. Now it is the custom for those who get a pardon to give themselves up to prison. To avoid doing this, I returned to the Pope and begged for a dispensation, but he answered that I must follow the custom. Thereupon I fell on my knees, saying that I would rather go back to Florence with his safe conduct to serve the Duke, who was waiting for me impatiently. On hearing this, the Pope agreed to give me the pardon without my going first to prison. The document was drawn up and his Holiness signed it. It was then registered at the Capitol. Afterward, on the feast day appointed, I walked in the procession very honorably between two gentlemen and so was cleared at last.

In Rome I finished Duke Alessandro's medal in steel, and it was the finest work of its kind I had ever produced. When it was finished, I was instructed to bring it without hesitation to Florence to the Duke. But soon the news reached Rome of Duke Alessandro's death. Not long thereafter Cosimo de' Medici was made Duke.

About this time the Emperor Charles V returned victorious from his expedition against Tunis and the Pope sent for me to ask my advice concerning a present of honor fit to give him. I answered that it seemed to me most appropriate to present his Imperial Majesty with a golden crucifix, for which I had almost finished an ornament. I had already made three little figures of gold in the round, about a palm high, which I had begun for the chalice of Pope Clement, representing Faith, Hope and Charity. To these I added Christ in wax and many other exquisite decorations which gave the Pope complete satisfaction. Before I took leave of his Holiness, we had agreed on every detail and calculated the price of the work.

The next morning everything we had arranged was altered. The Pope told me that they wanted to make use of a Book of Hours of Our Lady, which was marvelously

When Duke Alessandro was murdered by his young cousin
Lorenzino, the elder branch of the Medicis became extinct.
Cosimo I de' Medici, not yet eighteen years old, seized the
ducal throne.

Cellini: missal cover for a French princess

illustrated and had cost the Cardinal de' Medici more than 2000 crowns. They thought this an appropriate present to the Empress and that for the Emperor afterward they would make what I had suggested. But now there was no time to lose since the Emperor was expected in Rome in about a month and a half. He wanted the book to be enclosed in a case of massive gold, richly worked and adorned with jewels valued at about 6000 crowns. In a few days I gave it so much beauty that the Pope was astonished.

I had nearly brought the work to completion when the Emperor arrived and numerous triumphal arches of great magnificence were erected in his honor. Immediately after his arrival he gave the Pope a diamond which he had bought for 12,000 crowns, which the Pope committed to my care, ordering me to make a ring for his finger. Then the Pope asked my advice concerning an apology which could reasonably be made to the Emperor for the unfinished condition of my work. I said a recent illness of mine would furnish a sound excuse, since his Majesty, seeing how thin and pale I was, would very readily believe and accept it. His Holiness added that, when I presented the book to the Emperor, I should say also that I made him a present of myself.

When I presented the gift to the Emperor, his Majesty graciously responded, "The book is acceptable to me and so are you. But I desire you to complete it for me in Rome. When it is finished and you are restored to health, bring it to me and come to see me."

I then set my hand with diligence to finishing the diamond ring for the Pope, and I took the ring to the palace, where the doors were always open to me. The Pope praised me in the presence of his household, wherein was a man who had become my enemy and assiduously strove to do me hurt. He put in his word: "There is no doubt at all that Benvenuto is a person of very remarkable genius, but still he ought to consider maturely what language it is right and proper to use when speaking of a Pope. He has had the audacity to say that Pope Clement was the hand-

Emperor Charles V, right, and Pope Paul III

somest sovereign that ever reigned and no less gifted; only that luck was always against him. He says that your Holiness is quite the opposite, that the tiara seems to weep for rage on your head and that you look like a truss of straw with clothes on, and that there is nothing in you except good luck."

These words registered with the Pope, though, far from having uttered them, such thoughts had never even come into my head. The Pope passed this slander off with a laugh, but nevertheless he harbored in his heart a deep vindictive feeling against me, of which I was not slow to be made aware, since I had no longer the same easy access to his apartments. On making dexterous inquiry I was told the story, but not the name of my calumniator. I could not imagine who he was. Had I but found him out, my vengeance would not have been trifling.

When I finished the book, I begged the Pope to send me with it to the Emperor as he had promised. Instead, I was paid very poorly for the book and for the diamond ring as well. I took what I could get and made up my mind to leave Rome without permission. The Pope meanwhile sent my book to the Emperor by the hand of his grandson, who told his Majesty that I had been prevented by illness from coming.

I finished my preparations for a journey to France, where I wished to go alone, but I could not do so because of a lad in my service called Ascanio, the handsomest youth in Rome, who possessed a marvelous aptitude for our art. I felt a warm and fatherly affection for him, even though he had run away from me to return to an old master and I had only taken him back because his father had pleaded with me. I had resolved to go to France, partly because I saw the Pope did not hold me in the same esteem as formerly, my faithful service having been besmirched by lying tongues. I was determined to seek better fortune in a foreign land, and wished to leave Rome without company or permission. But a Perugian workman in my employ begged me to let him go with me. Ascanio, who overheard

Cellini: medallion for Pietro Cardinal Bembo

this conversation, was half in tears, crying, "When you took me back, I told you I wished to remain with you for my lifetime." He was prepared to follow me on foot, so I engaged a horse for him too.

We began our journey toward France and crossed the mountains on the eighth of May; the snow covered them in masses. We arrived at Zurich, a marvelous city, bright and polished like a little gem; thence we reached Lausanne and Geneva, and from Geneva we came to Lyons, where we rested four days before setting upon the road to Paris. This was a delightful journey except for a brush with a band of adventurers who tried to murder us. It was only

Cellini's journey to France in 1537 was across the Alps, sketched earlier by Leonardo da Vinci.

Fontainebleau, Court of the White Horse

by great courage that we got free of them. From then on-
ward we traveled to Paris without the least trouble in the
world. Always singing and laughing, we arrived safely at
our destination.

After resting awhile in Paris, I was introduced to King
Francis by his treasurer, who took me to Fontainebleau.
I was granted a whole hour of very gracious audience.
Soon his Majesty's court moved to Lyons and I went along,
expecting on the journey to discuss some work of art the
King might have in mind. On the way I started a close as-
sociation with the Cardinal of Ferrara. By the time we
reached Lyons I was ill and my lad Ascanio was also down
with fever. The French and their court were both grating
on my nerves and I started to count the hours till I could
get back again to Rome. Seeing my anxiety to return home,
the Cardinal gave me money sufficient for making a silver
basin and a jug. So I and my lads took good horses and set
our faces in the direction of Rome.

In Rome I opened a new large and roomy shop, where
I accepted commissions from several noblemen and mean-

while began the basin and jug ordered by the Cardinal of
Ferrara. I employed eight workpeople and labored day and
night for the sake of honor and profit. Now the arrangement I had with that Perugian workman who went with
me to France was that he would discharge his travel debt
to me, as well as his expenses for clothes and other sun-
dries, by monthly payments. At the end of two months
the rascal decamped. I had no choice left but to have him
thrown into debtor's prison.

During this time there arrived a letter sent posthaste
by the Cardinal of Ferrara, which informed me that King
Francis was asking about me, expressing a strong desire
to have me in his service. The Cardinal wrote that he had
informed his most Christian Majesty that I would come
at once whenever I was sent for. I immediately replied that
I had more to do in Rome than at any previous time, but
that if his most Christian Majesty made a sign of wanting
me, one word of his, communicated by so great a prince
as his most reverend lordship, would suffice to make me
set off upon the spot.

five

After I had sent my letter [replying to Cardinal Ferrara], that traitor, the Perugian workman, devised a piece of malice against me. He informed one of the secretaries of Pope Paul's son, Signor Pier Luigi, who was then called Duke of Castro, that I was worth more than 80,000 ducats and that the greater part of this property consisted in jewels, belonging to the Church, which I had stolen in the Castle of St. Angelo during the sack of Rome.

It so happened one morning more than three hours before daybreak, I went abroad to take the air. On the very spot where I had assassinated Pompeo, I was met by the Sheriff, with all his constables, who came up to me and said, "You are the Pope's prisoner." They took me straightway to the castle and locked me in an upper chamber in the keep. This was the first time in my life that I ever smelt a prison. I was then thirty-seven years old.

After being kept eight whole days in prison, I was sent up for an examination. I was summoned into one of the great halls of the papal castle, a place of much dignity, where three examiners began first to question me in gentle terms, which they soon changed to words of considerable harshness and menace. When I heard their charges, I could not keep from bursting into a great roar of laughter. "Was it not your business, before you took me up, to find out what I had done with those eighty thousand ducats?" I said to them. "Was it not your duty to inspect the record of the jewels, which has been carefully kept for the last five hundred years? If you had discovered anything missing in that record, then you ought to have seized all my books as well as myself. I tell you for a certainty that the registers, on which are written all the jewels of the Pope, must be perfectly in order. You will not find missing a single article of value belonging to Pope Clement which has not been minutely noted."

While I was delivering this speech, they sat and listened in astonishment. All three went together to report to the Pope, who gave orders that all the records of the jewels should be diligently searched. In spite of the fact that they ascertained that no jewels were missing, they left me in the castle without saying a word more about it. Signor Pier Luigi felt also that he had acted badly, and to end the affair plans were set to contrive my death.

During this time King Francis received news of how the Pope was keeping me in prison and with what injustice. He therefore wrote, claiming me from the Pope as a man in the service of his Majesty. Such a demand was certainly one of the most honorable marks of favor which a man of my sort could desire, yet it proved the source of infinite annoyance and hurt to me. The Pope was roused to such fury by the jealous fear that I would tell the whole world how infamously I had been treated that he kept revolving ways in which I might be put to death without injury to his reputation.

The castellan of St. Angelo was a Florentine like myself. He was called Messer Giorgio, a worthy man, who showed me the greatest courtesy and let me wander freely about the castle on parole. He was well aware of how greatly I had been wronged, and he granted me conven-

The aged Paul III

*Sixteenth century police
reflected in a Biblical
fresco by Andrea del Sarto*

iences to keep working at my trade. My shop was still open, so Ascanio, my apprentice, came to the castle and brought me things to work at. I could not do much, feeling myself imprisoned so unjustly, yet I bore my adverse fortune with as light a heart as I was able.

I had won the friendship of the guards and many soldiers of the castle. Often they told me I ought to escape, offering to aid and abet me, but I answered that I had given my word to the castellan. One brave and clever soldier used to say to me, "My Benvenuto, you must know that a prisoner is not obliged to keep faith like a free man. Escape from that rascal of a Pope and that son of his, for both are determined to have your head." I had, however, made up my mind rather to lose my life than to break the promise I had given that good man, the castellan.

I had a companion in misery, a friar, who had been

arrested as a Lutheran. He kept perpetually reminding me that I was in no way bound to keep faith with the castellan, since I had become a prisoner. I replied that he might be right as a friar, but not as a man, who is bound to keep his word under all circumstances. Seeing that he could not undermine my honor by subtle sophistries, the friar hit upon another way of ensnaring me. Cautiously he began to ask what means I could use, if my jailers locked me up, to unlock my dungeon doors and escape. I wanted to show off my cleverness, and replied that I was quite able to open the most baffling locks and bars. The locks and bolts of our prison, I told him, would be as easy as eating a bit of new cheese. All too carelesly I showed him how simply I could do what I said. He pretended to pay little attention, but all the same he learned the lesson well.

As I have said, the worthy castellan let me roam freely over the whole fortress. Not even at night did he lock me in. Moreover, he allowed me to work with gold or silver or wax as I wished, so I labored several weeks on the basin ordered by the Cardinal Ferrara. For recreation I took to modeling in wax some little figures of my fancy. The friar stole a piece of this wax and proceeded to get false keys made, using the method I had heedlessly revealed to him.

Detail of guardsmen: a Biblical scene

Inner courts in the Castle St. Angelo

Unfortunately for him, the locksmith revealed the plot. Then the castellan came upon the wax I was using and recognized it as part of the escape plot. "It is true that this poor Benvenuto has suffered a most grievous wrong," he exclaimed, "yet he ought not to have dealt thus with me. Now I shall have to keep him under lock and key." Accordingly he had me shut up.

When I was shown the wax together with the model of the keys, I told the warden exactly what had happened.

The dream of flying fascinated many artists: Icarus *by Giotto and, facing page, Leonardo's design for a flying machine*

This made him arrest the friar and he gave me back the same freedom as I had before. But now that I realized how serious events could become, I began to think hard about my own situation, seeing that another crisis might arise when I should want to use my own ingenuity. I certainly hoped to have better success than the rascally friar. So I started a plan to have new sheets of coarse fabric brought me by my servants, while I kept the soiled ones and did not send them away. I cut the sheets into strips, a third of a cubit in breadth, until I had made enough in my opinion to clear the great height of the central tower of St. Angelo.

The castellan was subject to a certain sickness, which recurred every year and deprived him of his wits. The sign of its approach was that he kept continually talking, or rather jabbering, to no purpose. These humors took a different shape each year. One time he thought he was an oil jar. Another time he thought he was a frog and hopped about as frogs do. Another time he thought he was dead and demanded that he be buried. Not a year passed but some such hypochondriac notion got into his head. This year he imagined that he was a bat, and when he went out to take the air, he used to scream in a high thin tone like a bat, and then he would flap his hands and body as though he were about to fly. The doctors, when they saw the fit coming on him, tried to give him every distraction they could think of. Since they noticed that he enjoyed conversing with me, they were always fetching me to keep him company. At times the poor man detained me for four or five stricken hours without ever letting me cease talking. He used to keep me at his table, eating opposite to him, and never stopped chatting and making me chat. But during these discourses I, at least, contrived to get a good meal. He, poor man, could neither eat nor sleep, so that at last he wore me out.

He took it into his head one day to ask me whether I had ever had a fancy to fly. I answered that it had always been my ambition to do those things which offer the greatest challenge to men. Nature had endowed me with a good body, much better for running and leaping than most others, so I felt sure that I had the courage to try flying. The warden inquired what methods I should use. I answered that of all flying creatures, none was so apt a model as the bat. No sooner had the poor man heard me say the word bat, which recalled his own delusion, than he cried out at the top of his voice, "He says true, he says true. The bat's the thing. The bat's the thing!" Then he turned to me and said, "Benvenuto, if one gave you the opportunity, should you have the heart to fly?"

I said that if he would set me at liberty, I felt quite up to flying after making myself a pair of wings out of waxed linen. Thereupon he replied, "The Pope has bidden me guard you as though you were his own eyes. Since I know you are a clever devil who would certainly escape, I shall now have you locked up with a hundred keys in order to prevent you slipping through my fingers."

I reminded him that I might have fled many times but had been true to the word I had given him. I begged him therefore not to add greater evils to the misery of my present situation. Despite my entreaties, he gave strict orders to have me bound and taken and locked up in prison. On seeing that he could not be persuaded, I told him before all his servants, "Lock me up well, and keep good watch on me, for I shall certainly contrive to escape!"

No sooner had I been locked in than I went about exploring my prison to find the best way of making my escape. Soon I thought I had discovered how to get out of my cell. To climb down the lofty keep, for so the great round central tower is called, I had those new sheets of mine, which I had cut in strips and sewn together. Next, I stole a pair of pincers from a guard, with which to draw out the nails that kept the hinges of my door in place. The door was double and the clinching of the nails could not be seen, so that I had great trouble. But in the end I succeeded. To prevent the absence of the nails from being noticed, I mixed some rust with a little wax, making the same color as the heads of the long nails which I had

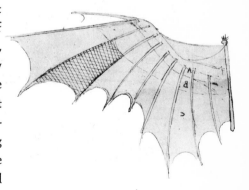

Cellini's cell in the Castle St. Angelo

extracted. I then made counterfeits of these nail heads and placed them where I had removed the nails. I left the hinges attached to their door-posts on top and bottom by means of some of the nails I had drawn, but I took care to cut these and replace them lightly, so that they only just supported the iron of the hinges.

It happened on the evening of a certain feast day that the castellan was seriously indisposed. His humors grew extravagant. He kept repeating that he was a bat and if they heard that Benvenuto had flown away, they must let him go to catch me, since he could fly by night most certainly as well or better than myself. "Benvenuto is a counterfeit bat, but I am a real one," he argued.

On the evening of that feast day, then, I made up my mind to escape, come what might. First I prayed most devoutly to God. Afterward I set to work and labored the whole night. Two hours before daybreak, with the greatest effort, I at last removed the hinges. Then the wooden panel itself and the bolt offered so much resistance that I could not open the door. I had to cut into the wood, yet in the end I got it open. Shouldering the strips of linen, which I rolled up like a bundle of flax on two sticks, I went forth and directed my steps toward the washrooms of the keep. There were two tiles in the ceiling through which I was able to clamber up onto the roof. I wore a white doublet, a pair of white hose and a pair of half boots, into which I had stuck a poniard I had managed to keep.

After scaling the roof, I took one end of my linen roll and attached it to a piece of antique tile which was built into the fortress wall. It happened to jut out scarcely four fingers. To fix the band I made it into the form of a stirrup. I attached it to the piece of tile, whispered a prayer to God and let myself go gently by degrees, supporting myself with the strength of my arms until I touched the ground. There was no moonlight but the light of a fair open heaven. When I stood upon my feet on solid earth, I looked up at the vast height which I had descended and went gladly away, thinking I was free.

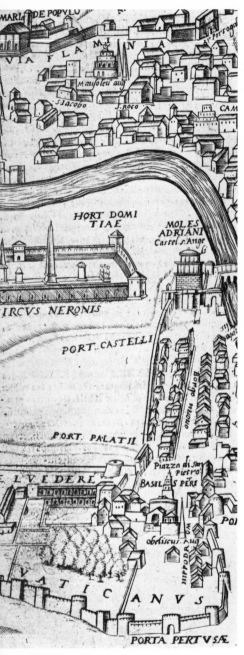

Cellini's escape route: from the Castle St. Angelo, upper right, to St. Peter's

But this was not the case, for the castellan on that side of the fortress had built two lofty walls, the space between which he used for a stable and a henyard. The place was barred with thick iron bolts on the outside. I was terribly disgusted to find no exit from this trap. But while I paced up and down debating what to do, I stumbled on a long pole, which I placed against the wall and then swarmed up hand over hand until I reached the top. But the wall ended in a sharp ridge, and I did not have enough strength to drag the pole up after me. So I made up my mind to use a portion of the second roll of linen which I had, the other having been left hanging from the keep of the castle. I cut off a piece, tied it to the pole and clambered down the wall, enduring the utmost toil and fatigue. I was quite exhausted and had, moreover, flayed the inside of my hands, which were bleeding freely. This compelled me to rest awhile, and I bathed my hands in my own urine.

When I thought my strength recovered, I moved quickly toward the last wall. There I put my bundle of linen lines down upon the ground, meaning to fasten them around a battlement and so descend the lower wall as I had the higher one. No sooner had I placed the linen than I became aware behind me of a sentinel going the rounds. I resolved to face the guard boldly. The fellow, seeing me advancing on him with a weapon in hand, quickened his pace and gave me a wide berth. My linen lines were some little way behind, so I turned hastily to get them back and came within sight of another sentinel, who also chose not to take notice of me. With my lines attached to the battlement, I let myself go. On the descent, whether it was that I thought I had really come to earth and relaxed my grip to jump, or whether my hands were so tired that they could not keep their hold, at any rate I fell, struck my head, and lay stunned for more than an hour and a half, as far as I could judge.

It was just upon daybreak when the fresh breeze which blows an hour before the sun revived me, yet I did not immediately recover my senses, for I thought my head had been cut off and fancied that I was in purgatory. With time, little by little, my faculties returned and I perceived I was outside the castle. In a flash I remembered all my adventures. I was aware of the wound in my head before I knew my leg was broken three inches above the heel. I bound my leg up as well as I could and crawled on all fours toward the city gate. I found it shut, but I noticed a stone just beneath the door which did not appear to be very firmly fixed. I set my hands to it and dislodged it. Through the gap thus made, I crept into town.

I had crawled more than five hundred paces from the

Square and steps of old St. Peter's

67

place where I fell to the gate by which I entered. No sooner had I got inside than some mastiffs set upon me and bit me badly. I drew my dagger and wounded one so sharply that he howled and all the dogs ran off. Meanwhile I made the best way I could on all fours toward the church of the Trespontina.

On arriving at the opening of the street which leads to St. Angelo, I turned off in the direction of St. Peter's. By now the dawn had risen and I felt myself in danger. By chance a water carrier came along, driving his donkeys. I called to him and begged him to carry me to the terrace by the steps of St. Peter's. "I am an unfortunate young man," I told him. "I was escaping through a window in an escapade of love when I fell and broke my leg." He carried me to the terrace by the steps, where I resumed crawling on all fours toward the palace of the Duchess Margaret, daughter of the Emperor, who had formerly been the wife of Duke Alessandro. There I should have been quite safe from recapture by the Pope.

But my exploits to this point had been too marvelous for a human being, so God chastised me a second time worse even than the first. While I was crawling on all fours, a servant of Cardinal Cornaro recognized me and ran to inform his master. The Cardinal exclaimed at once, "Run and carry him into my room here." When I arrived, he calmed my fears and sent for the first physician of Rome, who set the bone, bound the limb up and bled me. The Cardinal had me placed in a secret chamber and went off immediately to beg me from the Pope.

During this while all Rome was in an uproar. The bands of linen fastened to the great keep of the castle had been observed. Folk were running in crowds to behold so extraordinary a thing. The castellan had gone off into one of his worst fits of frenzy. In spite of all his servants, he insisted upon attempting a flight from the tower, saying that no one could recapture me except himself. Cardinal Cornaro threw himself upon his knees before the Pope and pleaded with him to pardon me. The Pope was shamed

and replied that he was sorry about my accident. He sent
word to me to take care of my health and that, when I
was recovered, he would make it all up to me for my
troubles.

Meanwhile the nobility of Rome, young and old, and
of all sorts, came to visit me. The castellan, out of his
mind as he was, had himself carried to the Pope and cried
out to his Holiness, "He escaped in spite of his word
which he gave me! Woe is me that he has flown away
when he promised not to fly!"

"I will give him back to you without fail," the Pope
said, laughing.

The castellan then asked the Pope to find out who
helped me escape. "If it is one of my men, I will hang him
from the battlement whence Benvenuto leaped," he said.

The Pope called the Governor, smiling as he said of
me, "He is a brave fellow and his exploit is marvelous. Go

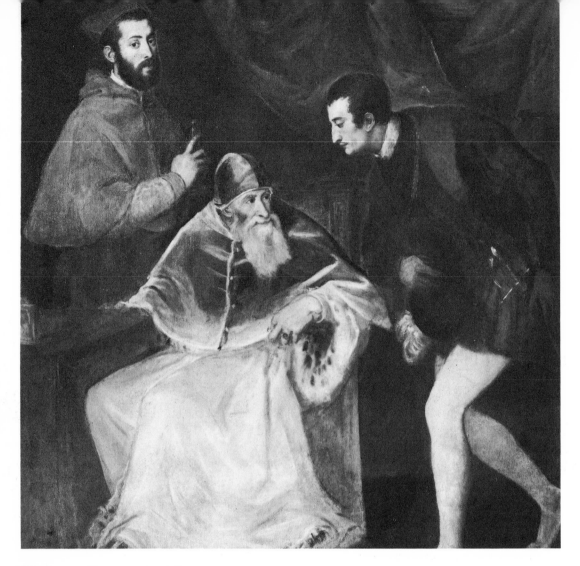

Titian's revealing portrait of Pope
Paul III and his nephews

and tell him to reveal his accomplices without apprehension since I have pardoned him."

So the Governor came and asked me to tell him frankly who had rendered me assistance. I related the whole story exactly as it happened, down to the water carrier who bore me on his back. When he heard the whole, the Governor said, "No man but you could have performed this exploit," and so he reported it to the Pope.

As chance would have it, Signor Pier Luigi, the Pope's son, happened to be present and heard all the company give signs of great astonishment. His Holiness remarked, "Of a truth this is a marvelous exploit!" Then Pier Luigi filled his father's head with a malicious tale that I had

fired my fowling piece at a cardinal and might fire upon
his Holiness, imagining that I had been so wrongly imprisoned. Pier Luigi charged me as being too quarrelsome and
too arrogant. The Pope swelled with rage but said nothing.
In truth, I had shot at a wild pigeon in a cleft high up
behind this cardinal's palace, without thinking of him or
any other person. On the contrary, I held the cardinal for
my very good patron. Let the world notice, when Fortune
has the will to ruin a man, how many different ways she
takes.

Two days later Cardinal Cornaro went to the Pope to
beg a bishopric for a gentleman in his service. The Pope
in turn wanted a favor from his most reverend Lordship,
which was to give up Benvenuto to him. The Cardinal
replied, "If your Holiness has pardoned him and set him
free in my care, what will the world say of you and me?"

The Pope answered, "I want Benvenuto. You want
the bishopric. Let the world say what it chooses." Feeling
a certain amount of shame, the Pope took what seemed a
middle course, offering to put me in those rooms which
opened on his private garden so that I could continue
my recovery and my friends could still come to visit me.

I begged the Cardinal not to give me up to the Pope.
I wanted to have myself wrapped up and carried to a safe
place outside of Rome. But the Pope heard about my plan
and sent at once and had me lodged in the ground-floor
chamber of his private garden. The Cardinal sent word to me
not to eat the food provided by the Pope, promising to supply
me with provisions himself. He urged me to keep up my
spirits, for he vowed to work in my cause until I was set free.
Thus I remained for some time until the night after the Corpus Domini, 1539, when the Sheriff came into my room with
a band of constables, strapped me in a chair and carried
me, all covered up, to the Torre di Nona, one of the worst
criminal prisons in Rome. There they put me on a wretched
mattress in the condemned cell. I could guess what my fate
was going to be. I turned my whole heart to God, devoutly
entreating Him to take me into His kingdom.

When day dawned, an emissary from the Pope came to pronounce my doom. I begged for a priest, for though I had already made my heart's confession to my heavenly Lord, I wanted to make peace with our Holy Mother Church. "Though she has done me this abominable wrong, I pardon her with all my soul," I cried.

The worthy man could not go on, but rushed to the house of Signor Pier Luigi's wife and entreated her, for the love of God, to tell the Pope to send someone else to pronounce sentence on me. Signor Pier Luigi's wife went to the Pope and threw herself upon her knees. She pleaded my cause so warmly that the Pope was put to shame; whereupon he said, "For your sake I will leave him in peace. You must know that we had no ill will against him." These words he spoke because of the cardinals who were around him and had listened to the eloquence of that brave, spirited lady.

Meanwhile my heart kept thumping against my ribs. My executioners stood around uncomfortably until the hour for dinner was past, then they took themselves off to their several affairs. A meal was also served me, which filled me with glad astonishment, and I prayed to God to save me from my fearful peril. An hour after nightfall the Sheriff arrived with his guard and brought me back to the castle from which I had escaped.

The castellan, ill and afflicted as he was, had himself carried to my cell and gloated over my recapture.

"Yes," I said, "but you see that I escaped as I told you I would. And if I had not been sold by a Venetian cardinal, in spite of a papal guarantee, for the price of a bishopric, you would not have caught me yet. Now you, too, do your worst. I care for nothing in the world."

The wretched man began shouting at the top of his voice. "Ah, woe is me! This fellow does not care whether he lives or dies. He is even more proud now than when he was whole and uninjured."

He ordered me thrown into a gloomy dungeon below the level of the garden. The cell was filled with water and

Sixteenth century prison scene

swarming with big spiders and many venomous worms. I was flung on a mattress of coarse hemp, given no supper and locked up behind four doors. The following day I requested some of my books to read and I was brought only two, one of them an Italian Bible. Thus, then, I continued to exist in misery upon that rotten mattress, which in three days soaked up water like a sponge. I could hardly stir because of my broken leg. When I had to get out of bed to obey a call of nature, I crawled on all fours with extreme distress. For one hour and a half each day a little glimmering of light penetrated that unhappy cavern through a very narrow opening. Only then could I read. The rest of the day and night I lived in darkness, enduring my lot and meditating upon God and the frailty of man.

I began the Bible from the beginning, reading and reflecting on it devoutly and finding in it deep treasures of delight. However, there was little light; and the thoughts of all my troubles kept gnawing at me in the darkness, until I often made my mind up to put an end to my own life. I was not allowed a knife, so it was no easy matter to commit suicide. Once I propped up a wooden pole, meaning to topple it over on my head and dash my brains out, but when I had arranged the whole machine and was just about to put it in operation, an invisible power took me and flung me away in such terror that I lay half dead. Afterward, when I searched my memory to find out what could have diverted me from suicide, I came to the conclusion that it must have been some divine power and my good guardian angel.

Around my prison I saw some scraps of rotten brick, from which by rubbing one fragment against another I composed a paste. Then, creeping on all fours, as I was compelled to go, I crawled up to my dungeon door and gnawed a splinter from it with my teeth. With these as pen and ink I began to write on some blank pages in my Bible a dialogue between my body and the spirits in my soul, which reproved me for wanting to destroy the handiwork of God and nature.

I continued reading the Bible, and my eyes became so used to that darkness that I could now read for three hours instead of a bare hour and a half. I spent the day singing psalms and other compositions on the theme of God's divinity. I was greatly troubled, however, by my nails which had grown too long and by my teeth which began to perish in my mouth. Nevertheless I accommodated myself to these new troubles. At times I sang, at times I prayed and at times I wrote, using the paste of brick dust. At this time I began composing a poem in praise of my prison, relating in it all the accidents which had befallen me.

The castellan used frequently to send messengers to spy on me and find out what I was doing. So it happened that I was overheard on the eve of the festival of August first, Ferragosto, praising my communion with God as happier for me than all the pleasures and frailties of the world outside. This so annoyed the castellan that he exclaimed, "Ah, God! That fellow lives and triumphs in his infinite distress, while I lack everything in the midst of comfort and am dying only on account of him. Go, fling him into that deepest of underground dungeons. Perhaps when he finds himself in such misfortune, his spirits will sink a little."

It was four months now that I had lain upon my back with my leg broken. I had so often dreamed that angels came and ministered to me that the limb now became as sound as though it had never been fractured.

Twenty of the castellan's servants seized me with force, roughly handled me and carried me away. They threw me in a hideous underground pit, which had swallowed many men alive. When they left, I began to sing. During the whole of that first day of August I kept festival with God, my heart rejoicing in the strength of hope and faith. On the second day I was taken back to my prison. The Pope, who had heard the whole story (and I must add that the doctors had already given up hope for the castellan), decided to let the castellan, before he died, take his revenge on me and put me to death in any way he liked. At first the castellan was bitter and cruel in his thoughts about me. At this point, however, the unseen being who had saved me from suicide came to me, still invisible but with a clear voice, shook me and said, "My Benvenuto, quick, quick! Betake thyself to God with thy accustomed prayers and cry out loudly, loudly!"

In sudden consternation, I fell upon my knees and recited my prayers. In an instant the same clear and open voice said, "Go, rest, and have no further fear!"

The meaning of this was soon clear. The castellan, after giving the most cruel orders for my death, suddenly countermanded them, saying, "Is not this Benvenuto the man whom I so warmly defended? Is he not the same man whom I know to be innocent? Instead of killing him, I give him life and liberty." This the Pope heard, and he took it with very bad grace indeed.

Visitation by an angel: fresco by Raphael and his School

To cheer me up the castellan furnished me with writing materials and wax, adding many words of kindness and courtesy. I began to work again. At that time the worthy man would have gladly granted me my liberty because he fancied that the great wrong he had done me was the main cause of his death. He pleaded with the Pope to grant my release, which the Pope seemed willing to do. It was Signor Pier Luigi, his son, who kept me by force. That day I was conducted back to the spacious rooms I had occupied the year before. There I obtained all the conveniences I asked for.

After the lapse of a few days, the castellan, who believed that I was at large and free, departed this life. The Pope meanwhile was letting me occupy my comfortable prison until he decided what to do with me. At that time the Pope's chamberlain engaged a soldier, who had been formerly a druggist, to administer a deadly poison in my food. They resolved to mix a pounded diamond in my victuals. Diamond is not a poison, but its incomparable hardness enables it to retain its very sharp edges. The diamond alone preserves its cutting qualities. If it chances to enter the stomach, it sticks in the coats of the stomach and bowels and after some time perforates the organs. This eventually causes death. When any other sort of stone is pounded, its fragments become rounded and blunt. They mingle with food but cannot attach themselves and so pass out with the victuals. Now the chamberlain gave a diamond of trifling value to a very poor goldsmith to be pounded into bits. The goldsmith returned dust which he said was the diamond properly ground down.

The morning when I took it, it was mixed with everything I had to eat. It is true that I felt the food scrunch beneath my teeth, but I was not thinking of knaveries of this sort. When I had finished, some glittering splinters caught my eye among the remnants of salad upon my plate. I rushed to look at them at the window and my eyes told me that they were certainly fragments of pounded diamond. I gave myself up without doubt as dead, and in my sorrow had recourse with pious heart to holy prayers. I was resigned. I blessed the world and all the years I had passed in it. At last I was returning to a better kingdom with the grace of God, which I thought I had almost certainly acquired.

But hope is immortal in the human breast. I felt myself tantalized by a gleam of idle expectation. Accordingly I took up a little knife and a few of these particles and placed them on an iron bar of my prison. I brought the knife's point with a slow grinding pressure to bear upon the stone and felt it crumble. In a moment new hope took possession of my soul. I rendered thanks to God and blessed poverty, for it had induced the goldsmith to keep the diamond and pound for me a greenish beryl of the smallest value.

The Pope was being pestered every day on behalf of the French king for my release, but he showed no disposition to give me up. Even my friends and patrons felt that

Titian: King Francis I of France

I ought not to count on getting out of prison for some time. I believed that I should get out in spite of them all.

A few days later the Cardinal of Ferrara arrived in Rome from France and went to pay his respects to the Pope, who detained him up to suppertime. The Pope was accustomed to drink freely once a week and then to vomit after his indulgence. When the Cardinal saw that the Pope was in good humor and ripe to grant favors, he begged for me at the demand of King Francis, pressing the matter hotly and showing that his Majesty felt strongly about it. The Pope laughed aloud. He felt the moment for his vomit at hand because of the excessive quantity of wine which he had drunk, so he said, "On the spot, this instant, you shall take him to your house." Then, having given express orders for this purpose, he rose from the table.

The Cardinal immediately sent for me, before Signor Pier Luigi could get wind of the affair. Two great gentlemen of the Cardinal's removed me from my prison and brought me to the Cardinal, who received me with indescribable kindness. I was well lodged and left to enjoy the comforts of my new situation. The Cardinal told me later that, had he not extracted me that evening, I should never have got out of prison. Indeed, he had already been informed that the Pope greatly regretted having let me go.

I cannot omit to relate another circumstance which is perhaps the most remarkable that has ever happened to anyone. Ever since the time of my religious experience in prison, an aureole of glory, marvelous to relate, has rested on my head. This is visible to every sort of man to whom I have chosen to point it out, but these have been very few. This halo can be observed above my shadow in the morning from the rising of the sun for about two hours and far better when the grass is drenched with dew. It is also visible at evening after sunset. I became aware of it in France at Paris, for the air there is freer from mist.

I stayed on for quite a while in the Cardinal of Ferrara's palace, where more visitors than ever came to see me. On all sides people expressed their admiration for me

Cellini: seal of the Cardinal of Ferrara

Cellini saltcellar: finished version of the wax model

and their astonishment that I had managed to survive such indescribable torments and to get out of prison. I quickly got myself ready to go back to work and was fortunate to find the silver basin I had begun for the Cardinal before I was imprisoned. Since the jug I had started was nowhere to be found, I began a new one for him. Both the jug and the basin were designed with round figures and bas-reliefs, in such richness of style that everyone expressed amazement at the strength of the design and the beauty of the execution. The Cardinal came to see me at least twice a day, and we passed many a pleasant hour together. Although I had plenty of work to do, he kept giving me fresh commissions. Among others, I had to design his pontifical seal, which was to be as big as the hand of a twelve-year-old boy.

In addition, the Cardinal asked me to come up with a model for a saltcellar, something new and different, something never attempted before. I conceived the idea

80

of portraying the intermingling of land and sea. On an oval framework I modeled two figures, considerably taller than a palm high, which were seated with their legs interlaced, suggesting those long branches of the sea which run up into the continents. The sea was a man, in whose hand I placed a ship, elaborately wrought in every detail, and well adapted to hold a quantity of salt. Beneath him I grouped the four sea horses, and in his right hand he held his trident. The earth I fashioned like a woman, with all the beauty of form, grace and charm of which my art was capable. One of her hands rested on a richly decorated temple, firmly set upon the base, which was intended for the pepper. In her other hand I put a cornucopia, or horn of plenty, overflowing with all nature's treasures. Below her I put the fairest animals of the earth. In the part presided over by the god of the sea, I fashioned choice fish and shells. The rest of the oval base I filled with luxurious ornamentation.

The Cardinal came to see my work, accompanied by two learned gentlemen. I produced the model in wax for them, and one of the Cardinal's companions, on beholding it, exclaimed, "This piece will take the lives of ten men to finish."

The other gentleman approved my effort, but the Cardinal then said that he did not care to start so big a project. I turned to the three of them and declared, "Most reverend Signor and you, learned gentlemen, I tell you that I shall positively complete this piece for the one for whom it is destined."

The Cardinal answered me in anger, "Unless you make it for the King of France, to whom I mean to take you, I do not think you will make it for anyone."

Then he showed me letters in which the King bade him return as soon as possible, bringing Benvenuto with him. At this I raised my hands to heaven and exclaimed, "Oh, when will that moment come?"

The Cardinal gave me ten days to put myself in readiness.

six

I might have traveled free of expense with the Cardinal, but I chose to take my own way by myself. I left Rome on Monday in Passion Week, with my apprentices, Pagolo and Ascanio, and together we pursued our journey toward Florence. There we dismounted at the home of my poor sister, who overwhelmed us with kind attention. Next we traveled to Ferrara, where we found that our lord Cardinal had provided us with all things necessary for our work. Later when the Cardinal arranged to leave for France, he let me know he was going without me.

I was very displeased, which led him to say, "Benvenuto, I am acting for your welfare. Before I take you out of Italy, I want you to know exactly what will be expected of you in France. Meanwhile, keep working on my basin and jug. I will leave orders here with my steward to give you everything you need or want."

The Cardinal then departed for France, leaving me behind in Ferrara, angry and dissatisfied. More than once I was on the point of taking myself off without a by-your-leave. The only thing that kept me back was the fact that

the Cardinal had obtained my freedom from Pope Paul. I set myself to work, therefore, on the jug and basin and made great progress. At that time the Duke of Ferrara sent for me to make a portrait of him, which I did on a circular piece of black stone about the size of a small plate. The Duke soon came to enjoy our conversations as well as my work, and not infrequently posed for me for four or five hours at a stretch, sometimes inviting me to stay to supper with him. It took me eight days to complete the seal with the Duke's likeness. For the reverse I modeled the figure of Peace in the form of a woman with a torch in her hand, setting fire to a trophy of arms. I portrayed her, with very thin drapery, in an attitude of joy, while at her feet, bound in chains, lay Fury in despair. The work won me the greatest honor with the Duke, who never tired of expressing his satisfaction.

While I was still working on the Duke's medal, the Cardinal of Ferrara sent me letters from France bidding me prepare for my journey since the King was asking for me. He wrote that his next letter would contain all the promised details of what I could expect in France. Accordingly I showed my jug and basin to the Duke and had them packed for the voyage. One day the Cardinal's agent sent for me in a great hurry, saying I must lose no time and take the post at once in order to present myself before the King, who seemed under the impression that I was already in France. I delivered my seal, which was by now finished, to the Duke of Ferrara, who treated me with the highest marks of honor and esteem. At the same time he told me not to leave Ferrara without informing him unless I wanted to incur his displeasure. As payment for the Duke's seal, he commanded his treasurer to give me a diamond worth up to 300 crowns. The miserly official found a stone worth a trifle over 60 crowns and proclaimed that its value was upwards of 200.

I had had enough of Ferrara and was wearying to get away from all its folk, for the Ferrarese are a very avaricious people, greedy of their neighbors' money. With-

Alpine valley in a storm, c. 1506, by Leonardo

The train of the French court

out further leave-taking, I set off upon my travels. The Duke, when he heard, was highly incensed and expressed a strong desire to make me come back. That evening I rode more than ten miles, always at a trot. The next day I found myself outside the Ferrarese domain and felt greatly relieved. Counting Pagolo and Ascanio and a servant, we were four men with four very good horses. We rode on until we arrived safely at Lyons, France, where we rested several days before setting off again toward Paris.

We found the court of Francis I, King of France, at Fontainebleau, where we immediately presented ourselves to the Cardinal of Ferrara. The Cardinal's basin and jug arrived the following day and the Cardinal then informed the King, who expressed his wish to see me at once. I went to his Majesty with the jug and basin. As soon as I was in his presence, I kissed his knee and thanked him for freeing me from prison. I expressed my feeling that princes of this earth, especially those as generous as his Majesty, were under special obligation to set free men of talent, particularly innocent ones such as I was.

The King listened to my speech with utmost courtesy. Then he took the jug and basin and exclaimed, "In truth I hardly think the ancients can have seen pieces as beautiful as these. I remember well looking at all the best classical works and all the masterpieces by the greatest masters of Italy, too, but I have never set eyes upon anything which stirred me to such admiration."

The Cardinal of Ferrara saw that the King was pleased by my arrival. He also judged that the little pieces that I had shown the King had encouraged him to plan some of

Hunting scene at Fontainebleau

87

Cellini: portrait medal of Francis I

the more ambitious things which he had in mind. At the time, however, we were following the court with much trouble and fatigue. The reason for this was that the train of the King drags itself along behind him with never less than 12,000 horses. In times of peace the train swells to 18,000 horses. As a result we had to journey after the King through places where sometimes there were scarcely two houses to be found. At such times we set up canvas tents like gypsies and suffered very great discomfort. I kept urging the Cardinal of Ferrara to suggest to the King that I be set up in some place where I could stop wandering and go to work.

One day the Cardinal informed me that his Majesty had made up his mind to let me start working. First, however, he wanted to come to an understanding about our arrangements. The Cardinal added, "It seems to me that if his Majesty allows you three hundred crowns a year, you will be able to keep yourself very well indeed. Furthermore, I advise you to trust yourself in my hands. I will work very hard in your interest."

I spoke up as follows: "When your most reverend Lordship left me in Ferrara, you promised not to bring me out of Italy before I understood the terms on which I should be placed here with his Majesty. Instead, your most reverend Lordship ordered me to come by post as if an art like mine can be carried on posthaste. If you had written to tell me that I was being offered three hundred crowns, I would not have stirred a foot. No, not even for twice that sum. Nevertheless, I am thankful to God and to your reverend Lordship for everything, seeing that God employed you as the means of freeing me from prison. So with all my heart I thank you and take good leave of you."

The Cardinal was greatly irritated and cried out in a rage, "Go wherever you choose! It is impossible to help people against their will!"

When I returned to my lodging, I found Pagolo and Ascanio and said to them, "Tomorrow I shall give you money enough to get you back home. For a long time an important business has been in my mind, and I mean to go about it now without you."

My horse was ready at dawn the next day. I divided everything which I had brought with me between the young men and 50 ducats of gold besides. I reserved the same sum for myself, together with the diamond that the Duke of Ferrara had given me, as well as two shirts. It was almost impossible to shake myself free from the two young men, who wanted to stay with me, come what may. I finally rode off and left them weeping. I took my way along a fair road through a forest, hoping to make at least forty miles that day and reach the most out-of-the-way place I could find. My mind was filled with despairing thoughts: never to show myself anywhere I was known and to forsake my art. My last work was to be a marble Christ which I had pledged when I was still in prison in Rome.

I had ridden about two miles when I heard horses galloping after me, which filled me with uneasiness, for the district was infested with a race of murdering brigands. However, the riders turned out to be Ascanio and a messenger from the King, with orders to bring me back immediately to his royal presence. The messenger informed me that he was ordered to take me by force if I could not be persuaded to return of my own free will. Ascanio, for his part, suggested that I obey because the King's practice was to keep a man in prison for at least five years before letting him out. This word about prison struck such terror in my heart that I wheeled my horse around and briskly followed the King's messenger to the court.

On our way to the King we passed the lodgings of the Cardinal of Ferrara, who was standing at his door. He called out to me, "Our most Christian Monarch has of his own accord assigned you the same terms which his Majesty allowed the painter Leonardo da Vinci, that is, a salary of seven hundred crowns. In addition he will pay you for all the works you do for him. For your journey here he gives you five hundred crowns."

Doorway at Fontainebleau

I replied that such offers were worthy of a great king.

On the following day the King ordered me to make models for twelve silver statues of gods and goddesses which were to stand as candelabra around his table. They were to be exactly as tall as he was, which was a trifle under four cubits in height. He told me also to go back to Paris and to seek out a place to live which would be suited for making the silver works he was ordering. He told me that he would see to it that I obtained any place I wanted.

In Paris I first set up shop in the Cardinal of Ferrara's house, where I began, in God's name, four little models in wax of Jupiter, Juno, Apollo and Vulcan. The King was very pleased with my work and commissioned me to complete the Jupiter in silver. I told him then that I had found a place which seemed to me exactly suited to my needs. It was his Majesty's own property, a little castle called Little Nello or Le Petit Nesle. It was in the possession of the Provost of Paris at that time, but he was not making any use of it.

An officer of the King took me immediately to the castle and put me in possession—not, however, without some fuss. The King's lieutenant warned me to keep a careful watch out for myself if I did not want to be murdered by the Provost of Paris, who was a great and powerful nobleman. I installed myself in the castle and immediately hired a retinue of serving men and put in a stock of pikes and other weapons. I must not forget to mention that I entered the service of his Majesty in the year 1540, which was exactly the year in which I reached the age of forty.

The castle was built in a triangle, right up against the city walls. It was quite old and of considerable size. I was counseled to look about for another place, because the owner was a man of vast power, who would surely have me done away with. I replied that I had come from Italy to serve the illustrious King of France and, as for dying, I knew for certain that die I must, a little earlier or later being a matter of supreme indifference to me. The King, informed of all these happenings, was deeply irritated and ordered that I be accommodated with all that I required. He did so in the most gracious way imaginable.

After fitting up the castle and the workshop with all that I needed for carrying on my business, I began to construct three models exactly as big as the final silver statues were to be. These were Jupiter, Vulcan and Mars. I molded them in clay and set them up on iron frames. The King, if I remember rightly, then disbursed three hundred pounds' weight of silver to get the undertaking started. While all these preparations were going on, we finished the little jug and oval basin and had them richly gilt so that they showed like the finest pieces of plate ever seen in France. The Cardinal of Ferrara presented them to the King, who was delighted with the gift. He praised me as no artist was ever praised before and expressed his intention of rewarding me further, but the Cardinal prevented him. It

Sixteenth century Paris, showing the Castel and Tour de Nello

would be tedious to relate all the knavish tricks of this prelate. I prefer to dwell on more important things.

In Paris the great favor shown me by the King made me the object of widespread admiration. The supply of silver was delivered and I began my statue of Jupiter. Many men were now working for me and, day and night, the activity was brisk in my shop. By the time I had finished the clay models of Jupiter, Vulcan and Mars, my workshop offered a grand show. The King came to Paris, and when he heard all I had been doing, he expressed a strong desire to visit me. Accordingly, one day after dinner, he set off with Madame d'Etampes, the Cardinal of Lorraine, the King of Navarre, his cousin, and the Queen, his sister. The Dauphin and Dauphiness also accompanied their father, making it the very flower of the French court which came to visit me. I was at home and hard at work when the King arrived at the door of the castle. He heard our hammers going and ordered his company to keep silence—so that his entrance took me by surprise. The first thing his Majesty saw was me with a huge plate of silver in my hand, which I was beating to make the body of Jupiter. One of my men was finishing the head; another was working on the legs. It is easy to imagine what din we must have made. The King seemed vastly amused.

On the following day the King sent for me and told me, very cheerfully, that since he had such a fine basin and jug of my workmanship, he wanted an equally handsome saltcellar to match them.

"Your Majesty," I replied, "while I was making the basin, I thought there ought to be a saltcellar to go with it, so I have already designed one. If it is your pleasure, I will show it to you at once."

The King said he would gladly see my model, whereupon I set off and returned in a few minutes with the wax model which I had made in Rome at the request of the

Detail of a goldsmith's shop

Cardinal of Ferrara. When I uncovered my piece, the King cried out in astonishment, "This is a hundred times more divine a thing than I had ever dreamed of!"

He told me he wished to execute it in gold and asked how much of the precious metal would be required. A thousand crowns, I answered. He ordered his treasurer to give me that very day a thousand old crowns of the truest weight.

It was still early in the day, so I thought I could conclude the whole business of the gold coins by daylight, without taking any of my workmen away from their tasks. I set off alone for the house of the King's treasurer, luckily carrying a small handbasket and not a bag. The thief of a treasurer, however, delayed paying out the money to me until three hours after nightfall. I tried to get word to my workmen to come and accompany me, but the messenger I sent was a rascal, who reported to me that my men had told him they were busy and could not come.

When the money was finally counted out, I put the pieces in my little basket and then thrust my arm through the two handles, holding in the gold securely. I could carry it this way much more conveniently than if I had a bag. I was well armed with shirt and sleeves of mail and my sword and dagger at my side. I made off with my basketful of gold as quickly as my two legs would carry me. With all haste I walked past the Bridge of the Exchange [now the Pont Neuf] along a wall beside the river which led to my lodgings in the castle. I had just come to the Augustins when I saw four men, swords in hand, advancing to attack me. I covered the basket with my cape, drew my sword and cried out, "All you can hope to get from a poor soldier is his cape and sword, and there will be little enough of these left before I give them up to you."

Then I crossed swords boldly with the four desperadoes. I spread out my arms to fool them into believing that I was not carrying any basket of money. The encounter ended soon. The ruffians retired step by step, probably

Cellini's route across the bridge and along the Quai des Augustins

saying to themselves, "This is certainly not the man we are after, or if it is he, he is not carrying anything." I kept harrying them with thrust and slash so hotly that I narrowly missed killing one or another. The four drew together and began to fall back. I quickened my pace, and when I was at a distance of a hundred paces from my house, I ran with all my might and shouted at the top of my voice: "To arms, to arms! Out with you, out with you! I am being murdered!"

Four of my young men came running, with pikes in their hands, and my adversaries took to flight. My men and I sat down together and supped with mirth and gladness.

On the morning following these events I began working on the great saltcellar, while pressing forward also my other pieces. I saw that I had silver to spare from the Jupiter, so I undertook a big two-handled vase without

consulting the King. I also made up my mind to cast the
large model of the Jupiter in bronze. Having up to this
date done nothing of this kind, I conferred with certain
old men in Paris, who were experienced in the art of casting in bronze. I described to them the methods in use in
Italy. They informed me that they had never worked in
the way I described, but if they could act on their own
principles, they were confident that they would bring the
bronze out as clean and perfect as the clay. I struck a
bargain with them, throwing on them the responsibility
and promising a bonus of several extra crowns.

The old men started the work going, but I soon saw
that they were going about it all wrong. On my own then
I began a head of Julius Caesar, bust and armor, much
larger than life, which I copied from a classic portrait. I
also started another head, modeled from a very handsome

young girl. I called this delightful work Fontainebleau, in honor of the palace in which the King took such delight.

We constructed an admirable little furnace for casting the bronzes, got all things in readiness and baked our molds. The French masters looked after the Jupiter and I supervised the other two heads. I could not help telling the men that I did not think they would succeed with the Jupiter because they had not provided sufficient vents for the air to circulate. They replied that if their work proved a failure, they would pay back the money I had given on account, as well as all other expenses which I had incurred. So they put the Jupiter into the furnace, while I placed the two heads, one on either side of the Jupiter. The metal melted down all right, and we let it flow into the mold with joy and gladness. The metal filled the mold of the Jupiter admirably and likewise the molds of the two heads. I was not sorry to have been wrong in my predictions about their work and they seemed delighted at the success of mine.

At daybreak they began quietly to break into the pit of the furnace. First they had to extract my two bronze heads, which came out in excellent condition. They set them up where they could easily be seen. Next they went after the Jupiter and had dug down scarcely two cubits when they set up such an outcry that they woke me up. At first I thought it was a shout of triumph and I came running. When I reached them, I found them downcast and terrified. Seeing my own two bronzes were all right, I tempered my annoyance. The old men prayed me to have pity on them, admitting finally that I had been right. They pleaded that they were in danger of being turned out into the streets abegging because of the loss they had sustained. I answered that if the King's treasurers insisted that they pay according to the contract, I would defray the cost out of my own purse, since they had tried to perform their task honestly and heartily, to the best of their knowledge. This offer of mine raised higher than I can describe my standing with the King's treasurers and other officers.

Junone

era istesa ejsecie
grāde piu del u

Cellini: sketch for Juno

seven

I shall now get on with the story of my life. I had on hand the following works, namely the silver Jupiter, the golden saltcellar, the great silver vase and the two bronze heads, all of which I have already mentioned. I also began to cast the pedestal for Jupiter, which I wrought very richly in bronze. It was covered with ornamentation, among which were bas-reliefs of the rape of Ganymede on one side and of Leda and the Swan on the other. I also made another pedestal for the statue of Juno, intending to begin that too if the King gave me silver enough for the purpose. I had also made several little things for the Cardinal of Ferrara and a small silver vase of rich workmanship which I meant to present to Madame d'Etampes.

On one visit to my house the King was attended by a crowd of his chief nobles and also his mistress, Madame d'Etampes. The King marveled to find how many pieces I had advanced and with what excellent results. Madame d'Etampes suggested to his Majesty that he ought to commission me to make something beautiful for Fontainebleau. I suggested several ideas and his Majesty expressed his own

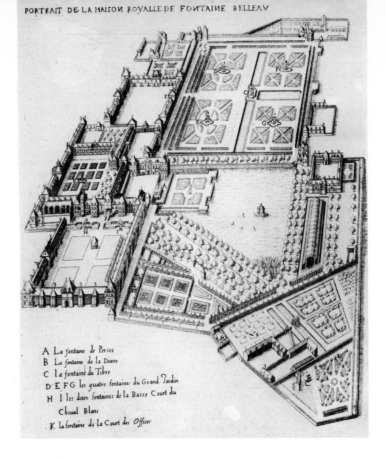

A La fontaine de Persee
B La fontaine de la Diane
C la fontaine du Tibre
D E F G les quatre fontaines du Grand Jardin
H I les deux fontaines de la Basse Court du
    Cheual Blanc
K la fontaine de la Court des Officer

Plan of Fontainebleau

opinions. Then he told me that he wished me to make
something in my richest style, seeing he delighted in the
residence at Fontainebleau more than in anything else in
his realm. So I took a model of a fountain in hand, at
which I worked assiduously.

For a month and a half, while the King was away
from Paris, I worked day and night to get my model so
well blocked out that my intentions could be clearly understood. Just about then the devilries of war were stirred
up again and I found his Majesty harassed by worries. No
sooner did the King hear about my models, however, than
he came to the place where I had set them up.

The first model was intended as a design for the
door of the palace at Fontainebleau. I had been obliged to
make some alterations in the architecture of the door,
which was low and wide in the vicious French style. I
corrected the proportions of the doorway and placed above
it an exact semicircle. On either side I fashioned two forms
which I call satyrs, though they showed only the satyr's

little horns and goatish head, all the rest being human. Above I placed a female figure lying in an attitude of noble grace, resting her left arm on the neck of a stag, one of the King's emblems. On one side I worked little fauns in half relief with wild boars and other game, while on the other side were hounds and various hunting dogs. The whole composition was enclosed in an oblong, each angle of which contained a Victory, in bas-relief, holding a torch in the manner of the ancients. Above the oblong was a salamander, the King's particular device.

When the King saw this model, it restored his good spirits and diverted his mind from the exhausting councils of war he had been enduring for the past two hours. Seeing him in such a cheerful frame of mind, I uncovered another model, which was a surprise to him. This model presented a fountain shaped in a perfect square, with handsome steps all around, intersecting each other in a way which was unknown in France, and is indeed very uncommon in Italy, too. In the middle of the fountain I had set a pedestal, on which was a nude male figure. In his right hand he raised a broken lance on high. His left hand rested on a scimitar. He was poised on the left foot, the right being supported by a helmet of the richest imaginable workmanship. At each of the four corners of the fountain a figure was sitting, raised above the level of the base and set off by beautiful emblems.

The King asked me what I meant by the fine fancy I had embodied in the design. I explained it thus: "Let me inform your sacred Majesty that the whole of this model is so exactly made to scale that none of its grace and lightness will be sacrificed if it should be fully executed. The figure in the middle is meant to stand fifty-four feet above the ground. It represents the god Mars. The other figures embody those arts and sciences in which your Majesty takes pleasure and which you patronize so generously.

"I have attempted to portray your Majesty, your very self, in the central statue, for you are truly a god Mars and use all your bravery with justice and piety."

The King called his treasurers and told them to lay out whatever I required, let the cost be what it might. Laying his hand on my shoulder, he said, "*Mon ami* (which is the same as 'my friend'), I know not whether the pleasure be greater for the prince who finds a man after his own heart, or for the artist who finds a prince willing to furnish him with means for carrying out his great ideas."

I replied that if I was really the man his Majesty described, my good fortune was by far the greater. He laughed and answered that we should agree that our luck was just about equal.

My luck, however, proved bad because I was not alert enough to play a similar comedy with Madame d'Etampes. That evening when she heard the story she became poisonously furious because I had not shown the models to her first. The King sought to defend me, but he made no impression on her bad temper. Hoping to regain her favor, I took the handsome little vase which I had made for her and presented myself at her house. Madame was still engaged upon her toilette and sent word scornfully for me to wait. I armed myself with patience, of all things the most difficult for me, and waited, keeping myself under control until the dinner hour came and went. By that time I was overcome with hunger and could hold out no longer. I went off, sending her most devoutly to the devil.

The story was repeated to the King, who laughed most heartily at Madame d'Etampes. This only increased her animosity toward me. Her vindictive rage grew and grew. She arranged with an Italian painter, a Bolognese named Francesco Primaticcio, who was known then as Il Bologna, to beg the King for the commission to do the fountain which his Majesty had already given to me. Madame d'Etampes added that she would support him with all her ability. With clever arguments, strengthened by Madame's mighty influence with the King, they hammered at the King day and night, and finally prevailed. What convinced him was the argument that I had not yet finished one of the twelve silver statues he wanted so much.

Duchesse d'Etampes, mistress of Francis I

102

Primaticcio: decorations for Madame d'Etampes' private apartments

"If you employ him on another great undertaking, you will, of necessity, deprive yourself of those other things on which your heart is set," they told his Majesty. "A hundred of the ablest craftsmen could not complete so many great works as this one man has taken in hand. One can see clearly that he has a passion for work, but his hot temper will lead to your Majesty's losing both him and his works at the same time."

Ce cy est la fontaine du Tibre qui est dans le Grand Jardin de la
Maison Royalle de fontaine Belleau au lieu Marque C. au portrait
dudit fontaine belleau

*The fountain of the Tiber, formerly
at Fontainebleau, featuring a
bronze by Primaticcio*

Influenced by these and other insinuations, the King consented to the petition, even though Primaticcio had at the time produced neither designs nor models for the fountain. For several months I heard nothing at all about this. During the same time the painter Primaticcio made no sign of beginning the work, keeping the matter very dark. When I learned how greatly and how wrongfully I had been betrayed, I made up my mind to handle the matter seriously and marched off with a good sword at my side to find Primaticcio.

Finding him in his room I began, "Messer Francesco, you know quite well that I was commissioned to do the great statue and that the time has long passed when my right could be questioned by anyone. Even so, I tell you now that I will be satisfied if you make a model, while I make another, and then we will both take them to our great King. Whoever's design wins out will deserve the final commission. Let us agree on this and we shall be friends; otherwise, we must be enemies."

"The work is mine," the painter answered, "I do not choose to put what is mine up for competition."

104

"If you will not do what is right, just and reasonable," I retorted, "I tell you plainly that if I ever hear you have spoken one single word about this work of mine to the King or anybody else, I will kill you."

The next day the man arranged to see me in Paris, and begged me to regard him as a brother, saying that he would never speak about that work again, since he recognized quite well that I was in the right.

If I did not confess that in some episodes I acted wrongly, the world might think I was not telling the truth about those in which I acted rightly. Therefore I admit that it was a mistake to inflict so unusual a vengeance upon my treacherous clerk, Pagolo. In truth, I believed him so utterly feeble, I should not have conceived the notion of branding him with such infamy as I am going to relate.

Not satisfied with having made him marry my faithless model, Caterina, I added to his punishment by inducing her to come back to pose for me as a model, paying her thirty sous a day in advance, plus a good meal, and requiring her to pose for me entirely without clothes. Then I took advantage of her, out of spite for her husband, and jeering at both of them. In addition, I kept her for hours in awkward and uncomfortable positions, which exhausted and irritated her. She was beautifully made, pleasurable to look at, and a credit to me as a model.

Caterina, noticing that I did not treat her with the same consideration as before her marriage, began to grumble and to talk big in her French way about her husband. The wretch piled insult upon insult till she goaded me beyond the bounds of reason. Yielding myself to blind rage, I seized her by the hair and dragged her up and down my room, beating and kicking her till I was tired. She swore she would never come back again, whereupon I saw that I had acted very wrongly, for I was losing a grand model, who brought me honor through my art. Moreover, when I saw her body all torn and bruised and swollen, I reflected

Cellini: Nymph of Fontainebleau,
after his "baggage" of a model

that, even if I persuaded her to return, I should have to put her under medical treatment for at least a fortnight.

On the following morning however, Caterina came to my door and fell upon my neck, embracing and kissing me and asked me if I was still angry with her. We partook of some food at the same table in sign of reconciliation and afterward I began to model from her. At last, just at the same hour as on the previous day, she irritated me to such a pitch that I gave her the same drubbing. So we went on for several days, repeating the old round like clockwork.

Meanwhile I completed a work in a style which did me the greatest honor. I cast it in bronze and the figure came out splendidly, as fine a specimen of casting as had ever been seen.

While this work was going forward, I set aside time for the great saltcellar and for the Jupiter. The saltcellar was soon completely finished, and I took it to the King when he came to Paris from Fontainebleau. It was oval in form, as I have already described, wrought of solid gold and worked entirely with the chisel. The piece rested on an ebony base, with a projecting cornice on which I set four golden figures in more than half relief, representing Night, Day, Twilight and Dawn. I included in the same frieze four other figures, similar in size, which represented the four chief winds. These were partly enameled with the most exquisite refinement. When the King saw the piece, he uttered a loud cry of astonishment and could not look at it enough.

At that time Primaticcio suggested to the King that he make casts of the great classical masterpieces, namely the Laocoön, the Cleopatra, the Venus, the Commodus, the Zingara and the [Belvedere] Apollo, which are, in truth, the finest things in Rome. The beast did not have the courage to compete with me directly, so he took the truly Lombard course of trying to diminish my work by becoming a copier of the ancient classics. It did not work out quite as he expected, as I will tell in its proper place.

That year, 1544, on the seventh of June, a daughter was born to me, whom I named Costanza. Her mother was the beautiful model with whom I put the finishing touches to the bronze Fontainebleau and also the two statues of Victory. I settled money enough upon the girl for a dowry and placed her under the tutelage of her aunt.

By laboring incessantly I had now got my various works well advanced. The Jupiter was nearly finished, as was the vase; the door too began to reveal its beauties. At that time the King paid me a visit and found the magnificent show of works finished enough to satisfy anybody's eyes. As he was inspecting these things, it came into his head that the Cardinal of Ferrara had fulfilled none of his promises to me, either of a pension or anything else. His Majesty ordered the Cardinal to pay me 7000 gold crowns at an early date, which the Cardinal said he would promptly do, but his own bad nature made him wait until the King's fit of generosity passed. With wars and rumors of wars on the increase, France was in great need of money. So the King went along with the Cardinal's argument to postpone the payment to me, though in his soul he knew that the Cardinal was acting not out of any care for the

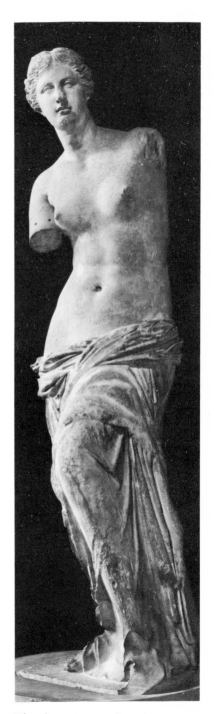

The classic Venus de Milo

107

Primaticcio: bronze copy after Venus of Knidos

finances of the realm but in order to curry favor. His Majesty seemed determined to reward me and ordered that the first benefice worth 2000 crowns a year that fell vacant should be given to me.

Madame d'Etampes, when she heard how well my affairs were going, redoubled her spite against me, saying in her own heart, "It is I who rule the world today, and a little fellow like this snaps his fingers at me!"

My silver Jupiter was now brought to completion, together with its gilded pedestal, which I placed on a small wooden platform equipped with four little round balls of hard wood, more than half hidden in their sockets. These were so arranged that a child could push the statue forward and backward or turn it around with ease. I took the statue to Fontainebleau, where the King was in residence. At this time Primaticcio had finished his copies of the classic masterpieces, which he had cast carefully in bronze. I knew nothing about this because Fontainebleau is forty miles distant from Paris. I asked the King where he wanted me to set up my Jupiter, and Madame d Etampes, who happened to be present, suggested the King's handsome gallery, a large hall of more than a hundred paces, where Primaticcio had already placed his antiques in a handsome row upon their pedestals. They were, as I have said, the choicest of the Roman classic antiquities. Placing my Jupiter in this grand parade, so carefully arranged, was like running the gantlet. I arranged my statue as well as I could and awaited the coming of the King.

My Jupiter was raising his thunderbolt with his right hand just in the act of hurling it; his left hand held the globe of the world. Among the flames of the thunderbolt I had introduced a torch of white wax. Now Madame d'Etampes detained the King until after nightfall, hoping either to delay his visit altogether or else to spoil the effect of my Jupiter by having it shown in the dark. But as God

The gallery of Francis I, Fontainebleau

has promised to those who trust in Him, it turned out exactly the opposite to her scheme. When night came, I set fire to the wax torch, which was higher than the head of Jupiter and shed light on him from above, showing the statue better than daylight.

At length the King arrived, attended by Madame d'Etampes, the Dauphin and Dauphiness [Henry II and Catherine de' Medici], together with the King of Navarre, his brother-in-law, and Madame Marguerite, his daughter. When the King appeared, I made my apprentice, Ascanio, push the Jupiter toward his Majesty. It moved smoothly forward and the gentle motion made the figure come alive. The antiques were left in the background and my work caught every eye.

The King exclaimed at once, "This is by far the finest thing that has ever been seen. I could never have conceived the hundredth part of its beauty."

Madame d'Etampes said boldly to the King, "One would think you had no eyes! Don't you see all those fine bronzes from classical antiquity behind there? Those contain the real distinction of this art, not this modern foolery."

The King continued to praise my statue, so Madame d'Etampes observed that my Jupiter would not make so fine a show by daylight; besides, she charged that I had put a veil on the Jupiter to conceal its faults. I had indeed flung a gauze veil over part of the statue, with a view to augmenting its majesty. When Madame finished speaking, I tore the veil off, leaving the god totally exposed. She took this action of displaying the naked statue as an insult to her. The King noticed how angry she was, while I was trying to force some words out despite my own fury. He stepped in, very wisely, and forbade me to utter a word. Unable to speak, I writhed in rage, which redoubled her irritation. The King left sooner than he otherwise might have.

I left the Jupiter there and departed the next morning for Paris, where now I attacked the great statue of Mars, which I had set up solidly upon a well-constructed wooden

Cellini's Jupiter, *bronze statuette, facing page; above, detail*

frame. Over this was spread a layer of plaster about an eighth of a cubit thick, carefully modeled for the body of the Colossus. Lastly I prepared a great number of molds for the figure, intending to fit them together according to the rules of the art. All the while I was also putting together the door, with all of its ornamentation, for the palace at Fontainebleau.

That accursed Madame d'Etampes seemed born to be the ruin of the world, so I should really consider myself important if she regarded me as her mortal enemy. She kept abusing me before the King until, to appease her, he swore to pay no more attention to me. The King's words were immediately reported to me by a page of the Cardinal of Ferrara. I was so angry that I threw my tools across the room and decided at once to get out of France. I dashed off on the spot to find the King, who received me graciously and asked whether I had anything worth seeing in my house. I replied that I had some pieces ready to show him if he pleased to come at once. He told me to go home and he would come immediately.

I went accordingly and waited for the good King, who, it seems, went meanwhile to take leave of Madame d'Etampes. When she heard where he was bound, she begged him not to go that day, so he did not come to visit me. The next day, seeing me again, he swore it was his intention to come visit me on the spot. But, as usual, he went to take his leave of his dear Madame, who, with her biting tongue, poured abuse on me as against a deadly enemy of the worthy crown of France. The good King calmed her by telling her that the object of his visit was to give me such a scolding as should make me tremble in my shoes.

At my house he was struck with such stupefaction at the great door, which I had put together, that he almost forgot to reprimand me as he had promised Madame d'Etampes. Still he wanted to find some opportunity of scolding me, so he began, "There is one most important matter, Benvenuto, which men of your sort, though full of talent, ought always to bear in mind, and that is that you cannot bring your great gifts to light by your own strength alone. You can show your greatness only through the opportunities which we give you. So you ought to be a little more submissive, and not so arrogant and headstrong. I remember that I gave you express orders to make me twelve silver statues and this was all I wanted. You have chosen to execute a saltcellar and vases and busts and doors and a heap of other things, which quite confound me when I consider how you have neglected my wishes and worked to fulfill your own. I tell you, therefore, plainly: do your utmost to obey my commands. For if you stick to your own fancies, you will run your head against a wall."

When he wound up with this sermon, agreed upon beforehand with his darling Madame d'Etampes, I bent one leg upon the ground, kissed his coat above the knee and said in reply, "Sacred Majesty, I admit that all you have said is true. I protest only that, day and night, with all my strength, I have been bent on serving you and executing your commands. Therefore I crave your pardon. I was under the impression that your Majesty had given me silver for one statue only, and since no more was put at my disposal, I could not execute the others. With the little surplus of silver I made this vase to show your Majesty the grand style of the ancients. As for the saltcellar, I thought, if my memory does not betray me, that your Majesty ordered me to make it of your own accord. You had a thousand golden ducats counted out for me to execute the piece, and what is more, I seem to remember that you commended me highly when it was finished. As regards the door, it was my impression that you gave orders that I obtain the necessary funds, because I should certainly never have been able to move so great an undertaking forward on my own resources. As for the bronzes, I cast the heads on my own account in order to become familiar with French clay. Without those experiments I could not have set about casting the larger works. I made the pedestals because I judged them necessary for the statues. So, in everything I have done, I meant to act for the best and never to swerve from your Majesty's expressed wishes.

"It is indeed true that I set up the huge Colossus to satisfy my own desire, paying for it out of my own purse, because I felt that I, an unimportant artist, owed it to a great king like you to erect a statue, the like of which the ancients never saw. Now, learning that God is not inclined to make me worthy of so glorious a service, I beseech your Majesty, instead of the noble rewards you have in mind for me, to grant me one small trifle of your favor and give me permission to leave. At this instant,

Cellini: detail of the completed saltcellar of Francis I, one of the few of his gold masterpieces extant

Peace concluded between
Charles V and Francis I, 1544

with your permission, I shall return to Italy, grateful to
God and your Majesty for the happy hours which I have
spent serving you."

The King then stretched out his hand to me and
raised me very graciously, saying I ought to stay in his
service and that what I had done was pleasing to him. My
indignation would not cool down so soon; I thanked him
respectfully, but repeated my request to leave. His Majesty
commanded me with a terrible voice to hold my tongue, unless I really wanted to incur his wrath. Afterward he added
that he was very well satisfied with what I had done and

ordered his secretary to pay me all the money I had spent upon the great Colossus, no matter what the sum, provided I wrote the bill out in my own hand. Then he departed, saying *"Adieu, mon ami,"* which is a phrase of familiar friendship not often used by kings.

But those devils, the English, were keeping us in constant agitation, and his Majesty had other things than pleasure to attend to. Several months passed without my receiving money or commissions, so I dismissed my work people, keeping only the two Italians, whom I set to making two big vases out of my own silver. I presented myself to the King, who was greatly delighted with the vases. Seeing him in such good humor, I begged him to grant me permission to travel to Italy. He listened intently, from time to time casting a terrible glance at me. He rose angrily from his seat and said in my native Italian, "Benvenuto, you are a great fool. Take these vases back to Paris. I want to have them gilded."

I approached the Cardinal of Ferrara and asked him to do me the favor of getting me leave to return to Italy. He agreed to do his best to get what I wanted and suggested that I might set out at once, if I chose to, because he would act on my behalf with the King. Since I knew that the King had put me under the Cardinal's sponsorship, his permission to leave was enough. I promised to come back on the slightest hint from his Reverence. The Cardinal told me to go back to Paris and to wait eight days. If the King refused to let me go, he promised that he would inform me without fail. If I received no letters, however, it would be a sign that I could leave with an easy mind.

I waited twenty days and began preparations to depart, which I did in my evil hour. After tarrying in Lyons for eight days, I resumed my journey, refreshed in strength and spirit, and crossed over the mountains into Italy without mishap. My heart was torn, one moment by my desire to reach Florence as quickly as I could, another time by the conviction that I ought to return to France. At last I made up my mind to take the post for Florence.

*Empty arch of the Loggia
de' Lanzi, Florence*

eight

The Duke of Florence at this time, which was the month of August 1545, was Duke Cosimo. I paid my respects, with no intention of accepting service under him, as God, who does all things well, had in mind for me. The Duke and Duchess questioned me about all the works which I had done for the King of France and I answered willingly and in detail.

The Duke listened to my story and commented that it confirmed what he had already heard before. Then he said to me, with great sympathy, "How small your recompense for such great works! Friend Benvenuto, if you feel inclined to make some things for me, I am prepared to pay you far better than that King of yours has done, even though you speak about him so respectfully."

I hesitated, expressing my deep obligation to his Majesty, who had freed me from prison and given me the chance to do some great works of art.

The Duke squirmed in his chair as I spoke, and hardly waiting for me to finish, exclaimed, "If you are at all disposed to work for me, I will treat you in a way that will astonish you, provided your work gives me satisfaction, of which I have no doubt."

I, poor unhappy mortal that I am, was burning with the desire to prove to that noble school of Florence that I was more than a goldsmith. I answered the Duke that I would be willing to erect for him in marble or bronze a mighty statue on his great piazza. He replied that, to start, he would like me to make a Perseus, which he had long set his heart on having. He begged me to begin a model for it at once. In a few weeks I finished my model, which was about a cubit high, in yellow wax and very delicately finished in every detail.

No sooner had the Duke seen the model than he praised it to the skies, saying, "If only you can execute this little model on a large scale, with the same perfection, Benvenuto, it will make the finest piece in the plaza."

I replied, "Most excellent my lord, on the plaza now are works by the great Donatello and the incomparable Michelangelo, the two greatest artists since the days of the ancients. Nevertheless, since your Excellency likes my model so much, I have the courage to make it three times as fine in bronze."

The Duke bade me set out my needs in a formal petition, detailing every requirement, which he would see attended to liberally. I am sure that if I had been cunning enough to secure by contract all I needed for my work, I should not have incurred the vast troubles which overwhelmed me as a result of my own oversights. But the Duke exhibited the strongest desire to have the work done and a perfect willingness to agree on the preliminaries. I did not see then that he was more a merchant than a prince, so I was open and frank just as if he were a noble, not a commercial man. I submitted a simple agreement, couched in the most general terms, which said: "Most rare and excellent patron, contracts of any value do not depend on words or written instruments. The whole point is that I should successfully carry out my promises in my work. If I do, I am sure that your Excellency will remember what

Cellini: Perseus *model in wax*

Cosimo I de' Medici, duke of Florence, and his circle of artists and engineers

you have promised to do for me."

The Duke and Duchess were charmed by the language of my petition and began to treat me with great favor.

I chose a convenient house, in a quarter which I found much to my liking, where I wanted to install myself and erect furnaces to begin working in clay and bronze or gold and silver, as required. The Duke ordered the house turned over to me. He entrusted the execution of his orders to his major-domo, who had been his tutor. I told this donkey of

Judith and Holofernes *by*
Donatello

a man what I needed, particularly for my workshop which I wanted to build in a garden adjoining the house. The matter was handed over to a paymaster, a dry and bony little fellow, with tiny spider's hands and small gnat's voice, who moved at a snail's pace. In an unlucky hour for me, he sent me enough stone, sand and lime to build a small pigeonhouse if I used the material most carefully.

This cold beginning left me discouraged and dismayed, but I picked up hope when I saw how much money was being squandered on ugly pieces of bad sculpture which were being turned out by that bull Bandinelli, my old master's son, who was to cause me so much trouble. I prodded the midget paymaster to make him move a little faster; it was like shouting to a pack of lame donkeys with a blind dwarf as their driver. On the brighter side, there was my old boyhood friend Tasso, the woodworker and carpenter, who helped make a wooden framework for the

Il Tasso

Perseus. Tasso, the best craftsman in his art who ever lived, was gay and merry by temperament. News came that my affairs in France were going wrong. In Florence my patron was lukewarm. But I found cheer with Tasso, who was always singing a falsetto song, and I drove away, as well as I could, the gloomy thoughts which weighed so heavily on me.

In the ground-floor room of my house in Florence I modeled in plaster my Perseus as big as the bronze would be, intending to cast it from this mold. But first I began the figure of Medusa and constructed a framework in iron. Later I put on the clay and baked it. I had no assistants for my work, except some shopboys. I was hindered from getting other workmen by Bandinelli, who told the Duke that I was trying to steal his workmen because I was incapable of setting up so great a statue by myself. The labor was enormous. I had to strain every muscle night and day. Just at that time my sister's husband sickened and died, leaving me the father and guardian of a distressed family of six girls of all ages.

Just about this time, too, the Duke commissioned me to make a golden belt, which I enriched with gems, delicate masks and other fancies. I was working in the Duke's wardrobe, where he came frequently to watch me work and to talk to me. I had clay brought and modeled a portrait of his Excellency, considerably larger than life, which delighted him enormously. He wanted me to move to the palace and set up my working quarters there, but I refused, assuring him that I would not be able to finish my work in a hundred years there. The Duchess also treated me with extraordinary graciousness and would have liked me to work for her alone, forgetting the Perseus and everything else. I, for my part, despite these favors which were being showered on me, knew only too well that my perverse and bitter fortune would not delay in sending me some fresh calamity. I could not forgive myself for my great mistake in leaving France.

Meanwhile I was making progress with my Medusa.

122

Cellini: bust of Duke Cosimo I

I had covered the iron skeleton with clay, which I modeled very carefully and baked well. Then I spread on the wax surface. The Duke often came to inspect the work, and became so worried that I would not succeed with the bronze that he wanted me to call in another master to cast it.

The first piece I cast in bronze was the great bust portrait of his Excellency. It provided much pleasure when it was completed, though my sole object in making it was to obtain experience of clays suitable for bronze-casting. I was of course aware that the admirable sculptor Donatello had cast his bronzes with the clay of Florence, yet it seemed

Cellini: bronze test casting

to me that he had encountered some enormous difficulties in finishing them. Since I thought that this might have been due to some fault in the earth, I wanted to make some experiments before I undertook to cast my Perseus. I learned that the clay was good, but that Donatello had not understood the material well enough.

Since I had not yet constructed my own furnace, I used one of a bell-founder for the bust of Cosimo, which came out sharp and clean. I set at once to build a little furnace after my own plans and design, and when it was ready, I went to work on casting Medusa, the woman twisted in a heap beneath the feet of Perseus. It was an extremely difficult task and I was anxious to become familiar with all the niceties of the art so that there would be no mistake with the great statue. The first cast of Medusa succeeded superlatively. It came out so clean that my friends thought there was no need to retouch it, but this is nonsense, in spite of the claims of certain Germans and Frenchmen that they can cast bronzes without retouching them. I hold that bronze, when it has first been cast, ought to be worked over and beaten in with hammers and chisels, according to the manner of the ancients and also to the custom of the moderns—at least those moderns who know how to work in bronze.

The result of the casting pleased his Excellency, who kept encouraging me by his interest. But Bandinelli kept whispering in the Duke's ears that my success with a single figure or two proved nothing; that I should never be able to put the whole large work together, since I was new to the craft. Bandinelli insinuated to the Duke that he was throwing away his money, which prompted his Excellency to withdraw that part of my allowance which was to pay for my work people. When I complained pretty sharply to the Duke, my speech made no impression. I was seized with sudden anger and a vehement emotion and addressed him:

"My lord, Florence has truly been the school of the most noble talents. Yet when a man comes to appreciate his own ability and has gained some reputation, and wishes to shed additional glory on his birthplace and on his prince, it is right that he should go and carry on his work somewhere else. To prove how true this is, let me remind your Excellency of Donatello and the great Leonardo da Vinci in bygone years and of the incomparable Michelangelo in our own time. They brought glory to your Excellency with their genius. I would like to play my part like them, so, my lord, give me permission to depart.

"But don't let Bandinelli out of sight. Give him everything he asks and more. For if he gets into the world, his ignorance is so tremendous that he will prove just the man to disgrace our illustrious school of Florence.

"Now, prince, grant me permission to go. I ask no other reward for all my work."

When the prince saw how firmly I had made up my mind, he turned to me with irritation and exclaimed, "Benvenuto, if you still want to finish the statue, you will get everything you need!"

I did get some slight assistance from him, but it was insufficient and I had to dip into my own purse to keep the work moving faster than a snail's pace. I stayed home most of the time and rarely went to the Duke's palace. I kept working with utmost diligence to finish my statue. I

Reclining woman, bronze by Cellini

125

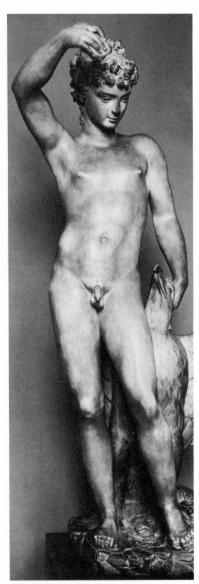

Ganymede, *restored by Cellini*

was paying my workmen out of my own pocket now, for the Duke withdrew his subsidy at the end of about eighteen months. I was in despair about my unlucky Perseus, and I wept to remember the prosperity that I had abandoned in Paris under the patronage of that marvelous King Francis.

Many days went by when I did not show my face at the palace. One morning the fancy took me to go there, and I found the Duke and Duchess had been discussing my skill in setting jewels. Her Excellency asked me to set a little point diamond in a ring for her, which I was eager to do. The ring pleased her and she afterward sent it as a present to King Philip. From that time on she kept sending me commissions and I did my best to serve her, although I saw precious little of her money in payment. God knows I had great need for money, for I was anxious to finish my Perseus and had engaged some journeymen whom I was paying out of my own purse.

One feast day I went to the palace after dinner and found the Duke in his wardrobe. He greeted me in a most friendly fashion and asked me to open a box which had been sent him. When I opened it I cried out, "My lord, this is a statue in Greek marble. I have never seen a boy's figure modeled so excellently, even among all the antiquities I have studied. I would like to restore this piece, with your Excellency's permission. I would repair its head and arms and feet and add an eagle, so that we can call the lad Ganymede. I don't usually bother to patch up statues, but the art of this great master cries out to me for help."

The Duke was highly delighted to find the statue so beautiful and plied me with questions about why my admiration was so excited. I tried to explain, as well as I could, the beauty of the workmanship, the consummate science and rare manner displayed by the classic fragment. I spoke at great length and with great pleasure because I could see that his Excellency was deeply interested.

While I was entertaining the Duke with my discourse, it so happened that Bandinelli entered the wardrobe.

Glancing at the statue in the open box, that great ox turned to the Duke and said, "My lord, this exactly illustrates the truth of what I have often told your Excellency. The ancients were wholly ignorant of anatomy, and their works, therefore, abound in mistakes."

I held my tongue. Indeed, I turned my back on the brute's disagreeable babble. But the Duke exclaimed: "Oh, Benvenuto, here is the exact opposite of what you were just now demonstrating with so many excellent arguments. Come and say a word in defense of the statue."

In reply to the Duke's kind appeal, I spoke: "My lord, your most illustrious Excellency, you must realize that Baccio Bandinelli is made up of everything bad and he has never been any different. As a result, whatever he looks at, no matter whether the thing be of superlative excellence, becomes in his ungracious eyes as bad as can be. I am inclined to the good only, so I see the truth more clearly. Consequently what I told your excellency about this lovely statue is mere simple truth, whereas what Bandinelli said is but a reflection of the evil of which he is composed."

The Duke's entourage tittered among themselves at the thrust I had delivered against my rival. So Bandinelli began again to chatter, crying out, "Prince, when I unveiled my Hercules and Cacus, I believe that a hundred sonnets were written about me, filled with the worst abuse that could be invented by the ignorant rabble."

I replied, "Prince, when Michelangelo Buonarroti displayed his Sacristy of San Lorenzo, with so many fine statues in it, the most talented men of our admirable school of Florence produced more than a hundred sonnets, too, each trying to outdo his neighbor with praise for the masterpieces. So it is, just as Bandinelli's work deserved all the evil which was cast on it, so Buonarroti's deserved the high praise which was bestowed on it."

Bandinelli burst out with fury, "What have you got to say against my work?"

"I will tell you if you are able to hear me out," I

rejoined. "I won't, however, tell you my own sentiments but rather the sentiments of our entire virtuous school of Florence."

The brutal fellow kept interrupting me with disagreeable remarks, waving his hands and shuffling his feet so that I was enraged and spoke more rudely than I might otherwise have done. "Well, all Florence says that if you shaved the hair of your Hercules, there would not be skull enough left to hold his brain. It says that it is impossible to distinguish whether his features are those of a man or of something between a lion and an ox. His sprawling shoulders are like the two pommels of an ass's packsaddle. His breasts and the muscles of his body are not modeled on a man's but on a sack full of melons. The loins are fashioned from a bag of stringy pumpkins. Nobody can tell how his two legs are attached to that ugly trunk. It is impossible to say on which leg he stands. The right leg of Hercules and that of Cacus have one mass of flesh between them, so that, if the figures were separated, each would be left without a calf at the point where they touch. They say, too, that Hercules has one of his feet underground, while the other seems to be resting on hot coals."

When Bandinelli saw the amused expressions on the Duke's face and the belittling gestures of the company— they felt that I was speaking the truth—he let his insolence get the better of him and turned on me, screaming vile and unspeakable insults. The affront half maddened me with fury, but I recovered my presence of mind and turned it away with a jest. The Duke and his attendants broke into shouts of laughter, but you must know, gentle readers, that I was just putting on an appearance of pleasantry. My heart was bursting in my body to think that a fellow, the foulest villain who ever breathed, should have dared to insult me so atrociously in the presence of so great a

Bandinelli's Hercules and Cacus: *Cellini's opinion has been generally accepted.*

Bandinelli and Cellini face to face

prince. If the Duke had not been present, I would have felled Bandinelli to the earth.

In his anger Bandinelli then went back on a promise he had made to send me a piece of marble, but the Duke intervened and a piece of stone was brought to my house the next morning, which I began immediately to chisel. I was so eager to work in the marble that I did not finish my model as correctly as the art demands. I noticed soon that the stone rang false under my strokes, yet I got what I could from the piece—an Apollo and a Hyacinth, which may still be seen unfinished in my workshop. His Excellency had sent to Rome for a block of Greek marble for the restoration of the antique Ganymede, which started my dispute with Bandinelli. When the marble came, I felt it a shame to cut it up just for the head and arms and other missing bits of the Ganymede, so I provided myself with another piece of stone and used the Greek marble for a Narcissus, which I first modeled on a small scale in wax. Meanwhile I pushed the Perseus forward in spite of all difficulty, hoping to finish it and to bid farewell to Florence.

Having succeeded so well with the cast of the Medusa, I had great hope of bringing my Perseus through with equal success. I had laid on the wax, and I felt confident it would come out perfectly in bronze. The Duke came to visit me frequently, and on one occasion said to me, "Benvenuto, this figure cannot come out in bronze. The laws of the art do not permit it."

His Excellency's words stung me sharply, but I expressed complete confidence in my ability. I took the moment, however, to appeal to him for the help I needed, which made the Duke turn first this way and then that, as though he could not stand my pleading. All at once he cried out, "Come, tell me, Benvenuto, how is it possible that that splendid head of Medusa, so high up there in the grasp of Perseus, should ever come out perfect?"

"Look you now, my lord," I replied upon the instant. "If your Excellency really understood this art, as you say you do, you would have no fear about that head. There is

130

Cellini, marble sculptures: (*left*) Apollo; (*right*) Narcissus

good reason, however, to be uneasy about this right foot, so far below it and so distant from all the rest."

The Duke was irritated and said to some gentlemen in waiting, "I really believe that this Benvenuto prides himself on contradicting everything someone else says."

I explained patiently, expounding most convincingly on the nature of fire to ascend and on the workings of my furnace. I told the Duke that the foot could not possibly come out, but that it would be quite easy to restore it. I assured him that the heads of Perseus and Medusa, on the other hand, would come out admirably. The Duke listened, shook his head and departed without further ceremony.

Again I was abandoned to my own resources. I banished the sad thoughts which filled my mind and took new courage, convinced that when my Perseus was finished, all my trials would turn into the highest good fortune and the happiest well-being. I set to work, using all my strength and what little money I had left.

First I provided myself with several loads of pine wood. With clay that I had prepared many months in advance, in order to season it fully, I made for my Perseus a clay tunic (for that is the term used), which I protected with iron girders. Then with a slow fire I began to draw off the wax, which melted and drained through numerous air vents. When the wax was drawn off, I built a funnel-shaped furnace all round the model of my Perseus. I laid the pine wood on by degrees and kept the fire burning two whole days and nights until the wax was completely gone and the mold solidly baked. I then set to work at digging a pit, into which I lowered the mold by windlasses and stout ropes down to the very bottom, where I had it set firmly in place with every possible precaution. When this delicate operation was accomplished, I began to bank the sides of the mold with earth, leaving where necessary proper air vents made of little tubes of earthenware.

At last I felt sure that everything was exactly right and that the pit had been filled in properly and the air vents placed as they should have been. I could see that my workmen understood my method, which differed considerably from the techniques of all other masters in the trade. So, feeling I could rely on them, I next turned to my furnace, which I had filled with numerous pigs of copper and other bronze stuff, piled so the flames could play through them freely to make the metal heat and liquefy faster. I called out heartily to set the furnace burning.

The pine logs were heaped in and, with the good draft that I had provided, the furnace roared so hot that I had to run from side to side to keep it going evenly. The work was more than I could stand, yet I strained every muscle and nerve. To add to my anxiety, the workshop caught on fire and we were afraid the roof would collapse on our heads. Then, from the garden, a storm of wind and rain blew up and perceptibly cooled the furnace.

I fought these threatening disasters for several hours, exerting myself beyond my strength until I could stand it no longer. A sudden fever, of the utmost intensity, overcame me, and I had to go and fling myself on my bed. I dragged myself away from the spot, after entrusting the rest of the job to my assistants, ten or more in all what with master founders, handworkers, country fellows and my own special journeymen.

"Observe all the rules I have taught you," I said to my apprentice. "Do your best with all speed, for the metal will soon be melted. You cannot go wrong. These men will have the channels ready. You will be able easily to open the two plugs and my mold will fill like a miracle. I feel sicker than ever before in my whole life and I believe that this fever will kill me before many hours are past."

With despair in my heart, I left them and betook myself to bed, where I spent two hours battling with the fever, calling out all the time that I felt I was dying. While I was writhing in agony, the twisted figure of a man came into my room and, in a mournful, doleful voice, like one announcing their last hour to men condemned to die on the scaffold, he moaned to me, "Oh, Benvenuto, your statue is spoiled and there is no hope of saving it."

I no sooner heard the wretched shriek than I let out a howl that could have been heard from hell, jumped out of bed, and throwing on my clothes, strode out to my workshop, determined to make trouble. I found my workmen, whom I had left in such high spirits, standing around, stupefied and downcast. I spoke to them at once. "Pay careful attention, everyone! Since you could not follow

One of the earliest known representations of a foundry furnace suitable for casting large bronze statues

instructions without me, pay heed now that I am taking charge of the work myself. I want no contradiction from anyone. At a time like this I want your hand and your hearing, not your advice."

One man tried to interrupt to say that our enterprise was hopeless, but I turned on him with such fury that all the rest exclaimed that they would obey my least command as long as they had a breath left in their bodies. They must

134

all have believed that I would shortly fall down dead upon the ground.

I immediately went to the furnace and found the metal curdled, an accident we call "being caked." I ordered two hands to fetch me a load of young oak wood, which had lain dry for more than a year at the house of a butcher across the road. His wife had previously offered me the oak wood, which burns more fiercely than other kinds. As soon as the first armfuls arrived, I filled the grate under the furnace. The logs caught fire, and oh! how the caked metal began to stir under the fearsome heat, to glow and to sparkle in flames! The new, roaring fire intensified the conflagration on the roof, so I sent men up to beat the flames out. I ordered boards, carpets and other hangings to be set up to protect us from the violence of the rain in the garden.

The cake stirred and was on the point of melting. I ordered half a pig of pewter to be brought in, which weighed about sixty pounds, and flung it into the middle of the cake inside the furnace. We piled on more wood, stirring constantly with pokers and iron rods. The curdled mass began to liquefy. The dead had come back to life against the firm opinion of all those ignoramuses. Such strength surged through my veins that all the pains of my fever vanished.

Suddenly there was an explosion, accompanied by a tremendous flash of flame as though a bolt of lightning had struck in our midst. We were appalled with terror, I more than the rest. I discovered that the cap of the furnace had blown up and the bronze was bubbling up from below. I immediately had the openings of my mold cleared out and the plugs removed that held back the molten metal. But I noticed that the liquid metal did not flow as rapidly as usual, the reason being that its base alloy had been consumed in the fierce heat of the fire. So I sent for all my pewter plates, my porringers and dishes, numbering in all about two hundred pieces, and cast part of them, one by one, into the ducts and also into the furnace proper.

The expedient worked miraculously. My bronze was in the most perfect liquid state and in a moment my mold was filled. Seeing my work finished, I fell on my knees and with all my heart gave thanks to God.

I let my statue cool for two whole days before I began to uncover it by degrees. The first thing I found was the head of Medusa, which came out admirably. Next I discovered that the head of Perseus had succeeded no less wonderfully. I went on uncovering the statue and found that everything had come out in perfect order until I reached the foot of the right leg on which the statue rests. There the heel was formed, but the toes and a little above them were unfinished, which made me very well pleased because I could prove to the Duke now how well I understood my business. I lost no time in reporting to the Duke, who had already heard about the proceeding but who deemed my accomplishment even more astonishing when he heard the tale from my own mouth. We were then in the first years of the reign of Pope Julius III.

The head of Medusa, from the Perseus

nine

I must beg your attention now, most gracious reader, for a terrible event which happened.

One day I was conversing with the Duke in his chamber, and he showed more cheerfulness than I had ever seen in him before. When the Duke was called away suddenly, the Duchess came in and took a seat beside me. She showed me a necklace of large and really very fine pearls, which I called a very handsome ornament when she asked me for an opinion. The Duchess then told me that she wanted the Duke to buy them for her, so she begged me to praise the pearls to him as highly as I could. At this I disclosed my mind to the Duchess with all respect and told her that there were grave faults in the pearls and for this reason I could not advise his Excellency to buy them. The Duchess replied that, except for those trifling defects, the necklace would be worth twice what the merchant was asking. I still hesitated because I do not believe that pearls are gems like diamonds, rubies, emeralds and sapphires, which never grow old. Pearls are but fishbones, which in time must lose their freshness. The Duchess

The Duchess of Florence, wife of Cosimo I

showed signs of irritation and exclaimed, "I want to own these pearls. So, I beg you, take them to the Duke and praise them to the skies, even if you have to use some words beyond the bounds of truth. Speak them for me and it will go well for you!"

Much against my will I took those confounded pearls to the Duke and praised them as the rarest and most beautiful ever brought together for a necklace. The Duchess, meanwhile, was standing behind a door listening to all I said. The Duke responded to me in kindly fashion and I was emboldened to add even more color of truth to my lies. I was relying on the Duchess' promise to help me out if need be. More than 200 crowns were to be my commission on the bargain, though I was firmly resolved not to accept a farthing.

The Duke again addressed me with the greatest courtesy: "I know that you are a consummate judge of these things, therefore if you are the honest man I always thought you, tell me now the truth!"

I flushed up to my eyes, which filled with tears, and I said to him, "My lord, if I tell your most illustrious Excellency the truth, I shall make a mortal foe of the Duchess."

The Duke thereupon pledged upon his honor to keep my words in confidence, away from the ears of the Duchess, so I told him the truth, that the pearls were worth far less than the price being asked for them. We were talking in low voices so that the Duchess, thinking our conversation over, stepped forward and requested the Duke to buy the pearls. He refused, saying he would be throwing away his money.

"What do you mean, throwing your money away," she exclaimed, "when Benvenuto, in whom you place such well-deserved confidence, has told me they would be a bargain at over three thousand crowns?"

The Duke said, "My lady, my Benvenuto here has told me that the pearls are neither round nor well matched. Indeed, some of them are quite faded."

At these words the Duchess cast a glance of bitter spite at me and retired with a threatening nod of her head in my direction. I was tempted to pack off at once and bid farewell to Italy. But my Perseus was almost finished and I could not leave without presenting it to public view. But I ask everyone to consider in what a grievous predicament I found myself!

Two-thousand-year-old Etruscan bronze Chimaera, *restored by* Cellini

The Duke had given orders that whenever I appeared at the palace, I was to be admitted through his living quarters to whatever place he happened to be. The Duchess commanded the same servants to drive me away whenever I showed myself.

Meanwhile the merchant who was peddling the pearls managed so, by nonsensical stuff and by playing the buffoon, that the Duke relented and concluded a bargain for the necklace. From this we may learn how evil Fortune spends her rage against a poor right-minded man, and how that strumpet Luck can help a miserable rascal. I lost the good graces of the Duchess once and for all, and almost had the Duke's protection taken away from me. That wretched peddler earned a thumping fee for selling the pearls and won the favor of the Duke and Duchess as well. It is not enough in this world to be a man merely of honesty and talent.

During those days some antiquities were discovered in the countryside near Arezzo, among them a Chimaera, a bronze lion, and a number of little statuettes, also bronze, each of them lacking either head or hands or feet. The Duke amused himself by cleaning these statuettes with little chisels used by goldsmiths. I helped him on several evenings clean off some earth and rust, and then the Duke commissioned me to restore the little statues. He wanted me to work at it all day but I could not afford to leave my Perseus for so many hours of daylight. The Duke, therefore, agreed to let me come to the palace at nightfall.

I was now on such good terms with his Excellency that he treated me every evening with greater kindness. About this time he had new living quarters built, to which I was ordered to come by way of a private passage. After a few days, the Duchess took to using these private passageways for her personal needs, so that everytime I came, I inconvenienced her. Soon she came to hate the very sight of me. Notwithstanding all these discomforts and daily annoyances, I kept going to the palace. The

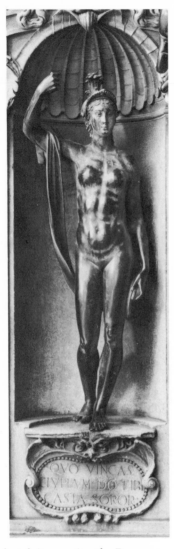

Pedestal figures for the Perseus:
*(left to right) Minerva, Mercury,
Jupiter; (facing page) Danäe with
the infant Perseus*

Duke's orders were precise, and no sooner did I knock
than the doors were immediately opened and I was allowed
to pass freely wherever I chose. As a result I would oc-
casionally come unexpectedly on the Duchess in a highly
inconvenient moment, which caused her to burst out in a
fury.

"When will you ever finish mending those statuettes?"
she stormed. "This perpetual going and coming of yours
has grown to be too great a nuisance."

I replied as gently as I could that the work on the little statues would last several months, but that, if she did not want me to come any more, I would obey her, even if the Duke himself sent for me. She made answer: "I do not bid you not to come, nor do I bid you to disobey the Duke. But I repeat that it seems to me that your work will never be finished."

One evening, after I had finished the small bronze figures which are worked into the pedestal of Perseus, namely the Jupiter, Mercury, Minerva and Danae, with the little Perseus seated at his mother's feet, I arranged them in a row, above eye level, which heightened their effectiveness. The Duke and Duchess heard of this and came to see them. They took seats in front of the statues and for more than two hours talked about nothing but the beauties of the work. The Duchess was so enthusiastic that she exclaimed, "I do not like to let those exquisite figures be wasted on the pedestal down there in the piazza, where they will run the risk of being damaged. I would much rather have them set up in one of my apartments, where they will be preserved with the respect due their special qualities."

I opposed her plan with many forceful arguments, but when I saw that she was determined, I waited till the next day when the Duke and Duchess were out riding. The pedestal had been prepared in advance, and I had the statues carried down and soldered with lead into their proper niches.

Oh, when the Duchess learned of this, how angry she was! I paid dearly for my daring. Her indignation about the pearls, and now about this matter of the statues, made her compel the Duke to abandon his amusements in my workshop in the palace. Consequently I stopped going to the palace so much. When I did, I found myself confronted with the same obstacles as previously.

I returned to the Loggia de' Lanzi, where my Perseus had been carried, and went on putting the last touches to my work, always plagued by the same old difficulty—

lack of money. When the Duke was informed that the whole of my work for the Perseus could soon be exhibited, he came one day to look at it. His manner showed clearly that it gave him great satisfaction, but nevertheless he said to some gentlemen attending him, "Although this statue seems in our eyes a very fine piece, still it has to win the favor of the people. Therefore, my Benvenuto, before you put the very last touches on, I should like you, for my sake, some day around noon, to remove part of the scaffolding on the side facing the piazza, so we may learn what folk think of it."

When the Duke left, I gave orders to have the screen removed, though some trifles of gold, varnish and various other little finishing touches were still lacking, which led me to murmur and complain indignantly and to curse the unhappy day which brought me to Florence. It was with deep ill humor that I unveiled part of my statue on the following day. But it pleased God that, in an instant, a shout of boundless enthusiasm went up in praise of my work, which consoled me not a little. The folk kept attaching sonnets to the doors, and I believe more than twenty, overflowing with the highest praise, were nailed up that very day. Even after I closed it off from view again, more sonnets arrived every day, including the highest praises from the artists, sculptors and painters of Florence. I placed the highest value on the eulogies of that excellent painter Jacopo da Pontormo and still more on those of his able pupil, Bronzino, who not only published his verses but also sent them by hand to my own house. So then behind my closed screen, I set myself to finishing my statue.

Now it pleased my glorious Lord and immortal God that at last I brought the whole work to completion and on a certain Thursday morning [April 27, 1554] I exposed my Perseus to public gaze. Immediately, before the sun had risen fully in the heavens, there assembled such a multitude of people that no words can describe them. The Duke was stationed at a window low upon the first floor of the palace, just above the entrance. There, half-hidden he heard everything that was being said about my statue, and after listening for several hours, he rose so proud and happy in his heart that he sent a message to tell me that he was delighted far more than he had expected and that he would reward me in a way which would astonish me.

Two more days passed by and the chorus of praise for Perseus swelled and swelled. I presented myself to the Duke, who said in good humor, "My Benvenuto, you have satisfied me and delighted me. I promise that I will reward

A bas-relief plaque by Cellini, originally at the base of the Perseus *pedestal*

147

you in a way that will make you wonder, and I do not mean to wait beyond tomorrow."

On hearing his most welcome assurances, I turned to God with all my body and all my soul and offered thanks to Him. I approached the Duke, almost weeping for joy, and asked him first to give me eight days to go on a pilgrimage to return thanks to God. This his Excellency was very willing to grant me.

I returned, and when the longed-for day arrived, I betook myself to the palace. As always, bad news travels faster than good. I was greeted with a wry mouth and a haughty voice by one of the Duke's secretaries, who asked me stiff as a poker how much I was asking for my Perseus. I was dumbfounded and astonished, and I replied quickly that it was not my custom to put prices on my work. The man raised his voice and ordered me, under pain of the Duke's displeasure, to say how much I wanted. I had been hoping not only for a handsome reward but even more for the good graces and favor of his Excellency, which is all I had ever sought. Accordingly, this unexpected demand for a price on my Perseus put me into a fury, heightened by the manner that venomous toad of a secretary took in talking to me. I exclaimed that if the Duke gave me 10,000 crowns, I would not be paid enough. The following day, when I paid my respects to the Duke, he turned on me angrily, saying, "Cities and great palaces are built with ten thousands of ducats."

And I replied, "Your Excellency can find many men able to build you cities and palaces, but you will not, perhaps, find one man in the world who could make a second Perseus!" I took my leave then without saying or doing anything further.

A few days later the Duchess sent for me and offered to help me settle my differences with the Duke, but I hesitated, which turned out that I had done the worst for

Cellini: Perseus

148

myself, because in spite of her angry feelings toward me, she could be quite generous. Instead, a friend who supplied the Duke's militia offered to settle the matter and I agreed, telling him anything would satisfy me provided I kept the Duke's good graces. I had heard a rumor that on several occasions the Duke had commented that for less than two farthings he would throw Perseus to the dogs and so settle any differences between us.

My honest friend was excellent in his dealings with soldiers, but he had no taste for statuary and therefore did not understand what had gone into a work such as mine. He concluded an arrangement with the Duke that I should receive 3500 golden crowns, which would represent not proper payment for my masterpiece but a kind of a token. Enough to say that I was satisfied. The Duke gave orders that I was to be paid 100 golden crowns a month, and so I was for some months. Then it fell to 50, later to 25, and some months to nothing. It is now 1566, eight years after I began this story of my life, and 500 crowns are still owing to me. There was also a balance due upon my salary, which I thought was forgotten, as it was not paid me for three years. But the Duke fell seriously ill, and finding the remedies of his physicians unavailing, he probably set himself to make his peace with God and ordered all his debts to his servants to be paid. I too was paid on this occasion, but I never obtained what was outstanding on my Perseus.

About this time a great block of marble arrived in Florence which was intended for a statue of Neptune. I knew very well that the Duchess had used her special influence to have the marble given to Bandinelli, but I felt I had to dispute his claims, not out of envy for him but rather out of pity for that poor unfortunate piece of marble. Observe, by the way, that if anything, no matter what, is doomed, nothing can save it from its evil end. It might fall into far worse, as happened to this marble when

Street scene, Florence

it came into the hands of Bartolommeo Ammanati, of whom I shall speak the truth in its proper place. I measured the splendid block from every angle and made several little models suited to its proportions. Then I presented myself to the Duke and persuaded his Excellency to set up a competition for the marble.

I spoke to him thus: "Arrange, my lord, that everyone who likes shall make a model. Have them all exhibited to the artists of our school of Florence. You will hear what the school thinks and your own good judgment will let you select the best. In this way, you will not throw away your money, nor discourage this group of artists who are unequaled anywhere else in the world and who form the glory of your illustrious Excellency."

The Duchess, who had already told me with great vexation that she wanted the marble for Bandinelli, tossed her head defiantly and muttered I knew not what angry sentences.

I eagerly set my hands to making my model for the Neptune and had hopes of winning the Duke's favor for it. I went to the Duchess and brought her some bits of goldsmith's work, which pleased her. Then I said to her, "My lady, I am working now for my own satisfaction on one of the most difficult pieces ever produced. It is a Christ of the whitest marble set upon a cross of the blackest. The whole piece is the size of a tall man."

She immediately inquired what I meant to do with it and I replied, "You must know, my lady, that I would not sell it for two thousand golden ducats. I bought the marble with my own money and have kept a young man for two years to help me with it. What with the stone, the iron framework which holds it and the wages, I have already spent over three hundred crowns, so I would not sell it for two thousand. However, if your Excellency will grant me a favor, I shall be delighted to make you a present of it. All I ask is that your Excellency not use your influence either against or for the models of Neptune the Duke has ordered for that great block of marble."

She replied with mighty indignation, "So you value neither my help nor my opposition?"

"On the contrary," I replied. "I respect them highly, princess, or I would not have offered you something I value at two thousand ducats. But I have confidence in my work and I hope to win the competition, even if it were against Michelangelo Buonarroti, from whom I have learned all that I know. Indeed, competing against such a sublime master would win me laurels in plenty, whereas there is little glory to be reaped in contest with lesser lights."

Bartolommeo Ammanati

The Duchess heard me out and then left in a half-angry mood. I went back to work on my model with all my strength. When it was finished, the Duke came to see it, bringing with him two ambassadors, one from Ferrara and the other from Lucca. They were delighted and paid me the highest compliments, especially the envoy from Lucca, who was a person of accomplishments and learning. I thereupon suggested to the Duke that he employ another admirable device to get the best result from the competition for the Neptune. My proposal was that the Duke order all competitors to make a model in clay as big as the block of marble itself.

"In this way you will be able to judge far better who deserves the commission," I said to the Duke. "And I might add that if your Excellency does not give it to the sculptor who deserves it, it will do less harm to the man but it will reflect great discredit on yourself, since the loss and the shame will fall on you."

The Duke shrugged his shoulders and began to walk away. I learned later that the ambassador of Lucca said to the Duke, "Prince, this Benvenuto of yours is a terrible man!"

And the Prince replied, "He is much more terrible than you imagine! It would be better for him if he were a little less terrible, for then he would have many things which he does not now have."

Bandinelli died several months after this, and it was

thought that, in addition to his intemperate habits, the shame that he would probably lose the marble contributed to his death.

Bandinelli had heard about the crucifix on which I was working, and he immediately laid hands on a block of marble and produced his Pietà, which may be seen in the church of the Santissima Annunziata. I had offered my crucifix to Santa Maria Novella and had already fixed the iron clamps to the wall. I only asked for permission to construct a little sarcophagus upon the ground beneath the feet of Christ, into which I might creep when I was dead. The friars hesitated about their consent, for which reason I refused to give the fruits of my enormous labors to the church and turned at once to the church of the Annunziata, where I was permitted to make my grave according to my will and pleasure. Bandinelli, learning of this, prayed the Duchess to get him the chapel of the Pazzi in the Annunziata for his Pietà, which was not altogether complete when he died.

Even as she had protected Bandinelli in life, the Duchess let me know she would protect him in the grave, and I need never try to get that block of marble. I had been given orders by the Duke to make a clay model of Neptune as big as the marble would permit, and then he had provided wood and clay and set up an enclosure in the Loggia near my Perseus in which I proceeded to construct a wooden framework according to my own excellent design. The Duke also paid for one workman. I brought my model to a conclusion, without caring whether I should ever do it in marble. Other contestants also worked on big clay models, including Giovanni the Fleming, Vincenzi Danti, a son of Moschino, and Bartolommeo Ammanati. One day the Duke, with Giorgio Vasari the painter, visited Ammanati's workshed and I heard that he was little pleased with what he saw there, in spite of Giorgio's trying to douse him with his fluent nonsense. He then asked if he could see my model, which I welcomed. No sooner did the Duke enter the enclosure and cast his eyes upon my work than he gave signs of being greatly satisfied. He walked all around it, stopping at each of the four points of view, exactly as the most knowing expert would have done. By nods and gestures he indicated his approval, but he said to me only, "Benvenuto, you should give a little polish to your statue."

One day, suffering intensely from food poisoning, I took to my bed. No sooner did the Duchess hear that I was ill than she succeeded in having that unlucky marble assigned to Bartolommeo Ammanati.

When I finally recovered and felt my vigor returning, I saw that I was being employed on nothing, and it pained me to lose the time which ought to have been spent on my art. I went to the Duke and entreated his most illustrious Excellency to dismiss me in a friendly spirit, so that I might not have to waste the few years still left me. The Duke did not take my request well and sent word that he would dismiss me if that was my will, but if I chose to work for him still, he would give me plenty to do if God granted me the strength to execute all he ordered. I replied that I desired nothing more than work and would rather have it from the Duke than from any man in the world, whether he was Pope, emperor or king.

I was then told, "If that is your mind, you and he have struck a bargain without need to say anything more. You need worry no longer. Just rely on the Duke's good will toward you."

Having quite completed my crucifix, I raised it some feet above the ground to show it off better. It produced a fine effect and I was so greatly satisfied that I exhibited it to everyone who expressed a desire to see it. As God willed, the Duke and Duchess heard about it and arrived one day quite unexpectedly, attended by all the nobles of the court. They were so delighted with it that each of these princes lavished endless praises on it, and all the lords and gentlefolk of their following joined in the chorus. Seeing how greatly they were taken with the piece, I thanked them with a touch of irony, saying that, if they had not refused me the marble for the Neptune, I should never have undertaken the crucifix.

"It is true," I added, "that this crucifix has cost me hours of unimaginable labor. Yet they have been well spent especially now that your most illustrious Excellencies have praised it so much. I cannot hope to find owners for it worthier than you are, therefore, I gladly present it to you as a gift."

Afterward I prayed them, before taking their leave, to visit the ground floor of my house, where I had my little model of the Neptune and the fountain, which the Duchess had never seen. She was struck with such force that she cried out with astonishment to the Duke, "Upon my life, I never dreamed it could be one-tenth so beautiful!"

The Duke replied, repeating more than once, "Didn't I tell you so? Didn't I tell you so?"

The Duchess later called me to her side and uttered many expressions of praise which sounded like excuses. They might indeed have been understood as asking for forgiveness. She told me then that she would like me to quarry a block of marble to my own taste and to execute the work. I replied that I would gladly put my hand to such an undertaking, no matter how arduous.

The Duke responded on the moment, "Benvenuto, you shall have all the accommodations you can ask for, and I will myself give you more besides."

With these agreeable words they left me, and I was highly satisfied. Many weeks passed, but nothing more was spoken of me. This neglect drove me half mad with despair. About that time the Queen of France, who was eager to complete a monument of her husband, Henry II, proposed that I enter her service, but the Duke would not let me go, saying he wanted me for his own employ. The result was that in my irritation I more than once made up

The fountain of Neptune by Ammanati—
the final fate of the contested marble

156

my mind to make off without asking leave. However, the Queen preferred to drop the matter for fear of displeasing the Duke, and so I remained here, much to my regret.

About that time the Duke went on a journey, attended by all of his court and his sons, except the prince, who was in Spain. They traveled through the Sienese marshes to Pisa. The poisonous air of those marshlands first attacked the Cardinal, who was taken down with pestilential fever and died after a brief illness. The Cardinal was the Duke's right eye, handsome and good, and his loss was severely felt.

I let several days go by, until I thought their tears were dried, and then I betook myself to Pisa.

The black and white marble crucifix by Cellini

chronology

1433   Cosimo de' Medici assumes unofficial rule of Florence
1464   Piero de' Medici inherits the family's authority
1469   Lorenzo de' Medici (the Magnificent)
1492   Piero II de' Medici
1494   Piero II expelled after ignominious surrender to French; the republic is re-established
1500   Birth of Benvenuto Cellini
1512   Cardinal Giovanni de' Medici restores family rule
1514   Cardinal Giovanni de' Medici elected Pope Leo X
1515   Cellini begins apprenticeship as goldsmith
       Francis I becomes king of France
1519   Cellini visits Rome for the first time
       Charles V elected Emperor
1520   Death of Raphael in Rome
1523   Cellini's second visit to Rome
       Cardinal Giulio de' Medici elected Pope Clement VII
1527   Rome sacked by army of Charles V
       Medicis again expelled from Florence
1530   Florence surrenders to Charles V; Medici rule restored
1531   Alessandro de' Medici named hereditary duke
1534   Pope Paul III elected
1536   Emperor Charles V makes triumphal entry into Rome
1537   Cosimo I duke of Florence after murder of Alessandro
       Cellini's first stay in Paris. Returns to Rome
1538   Imprisonment in Castle St. Angelo
1540   Released; enters service of King Francis I in Paris
1545   Returns to Florence; contract with Duke Cosimo I
1554   *Perseus* unveiled in Loggia de' Lanzi; Cellini admitted to nobility of Florence
1556   Cellini imprisoned in Florence on unspecified charges
1558   Cellini begins his autobiography; takes steps to enter religious order
1560   Is released from preliminary religious vows, marries Piera de Salvadore Parigi; a son and four daughters are born subsequently
1562   *Autobiography* breaks off
1564   Death of Michelangelo; Cellini chosen to represent Art of Sculpture in funeral ceremonies but is too ill to attend
1568   Publication of *Treatise on Goldsmithing and Sculpture*
1571   Death of Cellini; buried with public honors, Church of the Annunziata, Florence
1728   First publication of the *Autobiography* in Italian
1771   First English edition
1803   German translation by Goethe